# GARDENING FOR THE FAINT OF HEART

# GARDENING
## FOR THE FAINT OF HEART

Robin Wheeler

RAINCOAST BOOKS

*Vancouver*

First published in 2001 by

Raincoast Books
9050 Shaughnessy Street
Vancouver, B.C.
V6P 6E5
(604) 323-7100

www.raincoast.com

1 2 3 4 5 6 7 8 9 10

CANADIAN CATALOGUING IN PUBLICATION DATA
Wheeler, Robin, 1954–
Gardening for the faint of heart
    Includes index.
    1. Vegetable gardening. 2. Gardening. I. Title.
SB321.W54 2001            635            C00-911319-3
ISBN 1-55192-390-4


Illustrations: Bernie Lyons
Design: Bamboo & Silk Design Inc.

Raincoast Books gratefully acknowledges the support of the Government of Canada, through the Book Publishing Industry Development Program, the Canada Council for the Arts and the Department of Canadian Heritage. We also acknowledge the assistance of the Province of British Columbia, through the British Columbia Arts Council.

Printed and bound in Canada

# CONTENTS

# INTRODUCTION

## And yet another gardening book?

Sometimes, on answering a late-night call on my telephone, I will hear a barely audible voice, perhaps muffled through a handkerchief, asking, "Which way up do I plant a potato?" People in trench coats sidle up to me in parking lots and mutter queries such as "How do I move my rhubarb plant?" and "When should I water my carrots?" I get questions whispered over my shoulder in lineups, and bits of paper shoved into my hand by joggers on forest paths.

Who am I? I am The Woman Who Never Laughs at Silly Gardening Questions; I am the one who remembers all her own painful gardening lessons. And who are these folks, too embarrassed to reveal their agricultural insecurities, too timid to open up in front of their mothers-in-law, too nervous to enjoy or even start a garden? Who are they? They are the faint of heart. This book is for them.

## A gardening path for the faint of heart

Just as there are many successful ways to prepare those extra 87 zucchinis, there are an incredible number of paths for the gardener to take on the way to a healthy landscape. As a matter of fact, if you question 12 gardeners on where to put that rhubarb, or what and when to feed the raspberries, you will get 27 different answers, mostly because gardeners love to say "On the other hand ..."

Most of the answers you receive will be correct, because the earth is forgiving and will always meet you more than halfway. The particular answers in this book were chosen for ease of use, high sustainability quotient, low financial outlay and as examples of universal garden concepts. If you use these gardening ideas, you will have a healthy garden.

You will also be encouraged to experiment a bit, to put more importance on what you learned than what you produced, and to realize that there are many ways of doing everything. As soon as you feel confident with the information you have been offered, I hope you will investigate new ways of doing things. I hope you will feel encouraged to feel free and to have fun.

**Robin Wheeler**
*Roberts Creek, B.C.*

# WHY THE HECK SHOULD I GARDEN?

1

Here are 20 reasons why every person on the planet with a patch of dirt should start conscientiously tending it:

- Fruits and vegetables picked right off the plant are at their peak of flavour and nutritional value
- Growing and eating chemical-free foods is better for your health
- Grandma was right about eating a peck of dirt before you die! Soils contain naturally occurring elements that have been shown to boost the immune system
- Every ounce of fresh food from your garden saves you pennies to get ahead somewhere else

- If you are short of funds, you can now grow your own "gifts" — bouquets, dried herbs, seeds and food baskets
- When funds and spirits both are low in the middle of winter, you can roll some squash off the basement shelf, grab a jar of frozen tomatoes and phone your friends to bring over the rest of the ingredients for dinner
- You can learn how to make a "safe zone" for yourself out in the garden with an old chair and some flower boxes, and become renewed
- Being outside is always better than being inside, unless a tornado is coming, which is not likely
- Everyone looks better with a rosy glow and good biceps
- If you can run outside for that extra couple of potatoes when company comes, you have saved yourself some hysteria. You will feel smug!
- Kids who follow you around in the garden learn a lot about dirt, bugs, raw beans and having fun with their parents. Adults can learn about having patience
- Kids can learn by watching that they can have control over their environment in a positive way
- Gardening can offer you the Zen-like experience of eating a sun-warmed strawberry as you stand in your bare feet, listening to the distant drone of an airplane
- Gardening opens the door to other experiments in self-sufficiency, such as wandering up the bluff to pick berries for jam, or harvesting roots for coffee substitutes, or starting a herb business
- You can acknowledge your control (stewardship) over a tiny piece of the planet and run it exactly as you wish. Want a cleaner planet? Declare a chemical-free zone. Want butterflies and migrating birds to have a place to rest? Protect a wild area and re-seed their food plants. Just think what could happen if everyone on your street did this — on the block, in your town!
- Every time you feed yourself from your garden, you reduce the amount of pollution a truck would create bringing that food to your local store. You also eliminate your own pollution

and fuel costs by not driving to that store to buy that produce

- You are more likely to become "one with the universe" by gardening than by sitting on the couch with the TV remote control in your hand
- Gardeners tend to form into local "packs" to exchange seeds, plants and information. When they see your interest, from over the fence or in the garden supply store, you'll gain a whole new support system
- You can take your cumulative gardening knowledge with you anywhere you go. It will work all over the planet
- Learning to garden is like riding a bicycle — you can only get better, and you'll never forget how

## YES, BUT ...

### ... it will be hard to hack a garden out of this wasteland of a backyard

Do it in bits and pieces, getting sections of it under control before worrying about the rest. For instance, you could clear and plant the strip along the fence, or a patch by the compost heap, before trying something bigger. It will get easier as you go along and get the "feel" of turning and clearing the soil.

### ... I live in a rented house and never know how long I'll be there before they sell the place

You could put in a garden anyway, just for the experience. And who knows, you may still be there when things ripen. Putting in a garden may be wasted on your landlord, but perhaps not on the next owner or tenant. Good karma! Your other alternative is to "container garden." Lots of the smaller-rooted, quick-growing veggies will develop happily in a pot if you keep it wet enough. And if you start container-growing berry bushes and small trees now, and just move them with you, you'll have a pre-made garden for the first place you own!

### ... I don't have time to garden

Oh, poop! I bet if you wrote down all the hours of your day and crossed off the TV watching, the long telephone calls and the looking-out-the-window-with-a-cup-of-coffee, you'd easily have a couple of hours a week to maintain a veggie garden. That's really all it takes.

Once it's established, some watering (turning the hose on and off) and some well-directed weeding is all it will take to keep things going until you do have a chunk of time for a major cleanup. The funny thing is, once people get hooked they wonder why they once thought they didn't have time to hunker down on a sunny day and tend the plants. If you're busy or stressed out, tending the garden can become the most soothing part of the week.

### ... I have kids, and they'll eat all the stuff before I can pick it

Now, read that complaint again. "But, if I plant a garden, my children will eat all that fresh, organic food, for pennies a serving, and ... oh, that starts to sound kind of good!"

### ... I don't have enough money to start a garden

Money? How did that word creep in? The nice thing about gardening is that it can be done successfully for almost nothing. (See chapter 2, "Getting Started.") A packet of seeds is cheaper than a pack of cigarettes, and if you save the seeds from your plants, you may never need to buy seed for that variety again. One single pea seed's output will grow about 20 plants next year. A single broccoli seed, planted and left to grow out, will produce hundreds of seeds when it matures. The planet is wildly abundant, and gardening is one way to tap into that.

### ... vegetables are so cheap to buy, why should I grow them?

Growing your own food gives you a sense of control over your life you may not have felt for a long time. You eat exactly what you want and it's always fresh and healthy. You may have excess harvest to sell or give away, and that will make you feel good. And you can grow fancy veggies for the same price as cheap ones and raise your standard of living! I spent a weekend out of town visiting some friends who were having a bit of a bad spell and didn't have much money, but they did have a garden and they did eat in style! We had squash and beans and carrots, and canned chicken with lots of gravy, and big bowls of potatoes, and frozen peaches and apples. That was my first dinner at their house, and mealtime only improved after that. If you have some dirt around you, you can make a difference to how you live.

**... I only have a little tiny bit of yard. How can that possibly make a difference to my life?**
In China, many people in rural areas are expected to feed their families from a 20-by-20-foot gardening space. If you think hard about that, you'll realize how intensively these little gardens are used! This takes skill and experience, but any patch of dirt is certainly a starting point. The rural Chinese eat a lot of high-nutrient, fast-growing greens, so their choices are carefully made. It should make us feel spoiled, with our big lawns, to have no garden at all. There are lots of books to teach you about small gardens. See "Further Resources" for suggested reading.

**... I've seen my friends' gardening books and it will take too long to learn all the stuff I need to know to make plants grow**
Fortunately, people don't make plants grow. If you don't believe me, look at your local forest. Plants grow themselves; we only help them by making life more comfortable. You might need a bit of information to help plants grow well in your garden, but if you read this book you'll be farther ahead and ready to experiment. When and if you decide to get fancy, you can look at all those other books.

**... I have no garden space to use**
Nice try, but we thought of that! See chapter 2, "Getting Started."

**... I really hate getting dirty, and bugs bug me**
A lot of old fears slowly slip away when you find out you aren't normally harmed by what scared you. People who hate spiders actually get used to

having them around once they see them eating bugs in the greenhouse, or have time to enjoy watching one (from a safe distance) making a web in the bushes. When you learn that the insects aren't going to rush out and yell, and that the dirt will wash off, a more relaxed sensation will follow and that can permeate your whole life. Start soon!

As if it weren't enough to grow yourself some dinner, you can gain some skills that might help you get ahead financially and socially. This list is just the beginning:

- Grow winter vegetables to save money all year
- Sell excess veggies at the market
- Trade them for other vegetables
- Freeze them, dry them, can them
- Grow rare or endangered plants
- Grow berries or peppers to sell to your nearest cottage industry
- Heck, start your own cottage industry by making value-added products
- Grow and dry flowers
- Give flower arrangements as gifts
- Sell flower arrangements at your local farmers' market
- Grow edible flowers and sell them to restaurants
- Divide your plants and sell the extras at garage sales
- Grow plants to give to people who need them or just love them
- Sell vegetable seedlings at the market, or use them as a donation for a fundraiser — if they don't sell, plant them!
- Grow and dry herbs for home use, or to trade or give away
- Make dried arrangements to sell at craft stores
- Make tea blends
- Save your own seed to sell/trade/give as gifts
- Make herbal vinegar blends for Christmas baskets, or try some herb/honey combinations
- Be the community gardener and help your friends
- Teach kids about the different scents and tastes of garden herbs
- Offer fresh flowers to your local seniors' hall or hospital extended care unit

# GETTING STARTED

2

We will begin this chapter with the part where you sit in an armchair and think. We will then move to the section where you actually splash mud on your running shoes, and it will be a straight path to nirvana from there.

**My garden list**

- Hammock!!!!!
- Flowers for bouquets
- Salad greens
- Fresh herbs
- Herbs for drying
- Garlic for everything!
- Pumpkins for Halloween
- Bench

# SITTING AND THINKING

First of all, get comfy. Then get up again and find lots of scrap paper and a marking pen. Go back to your chair. Get comfy again. We're going to develop a loose, changeable plan for your garden.

## Mapping your garden

Quickly sketch out a map of your yard, marking in the house, outbuildings, fences and other permanent structures and scratching in the trees and existing garden areas. Mark in paths, too, and not just the existing, visible walkways, but the invisible one the dog takes to get to the garbage cans next door, and the one you use to get the lawnmower out of the shed. These "invisible" paths often make the most sense and are hardest to change through retraining. If you put a garden across those paths, there will be little footprints right where the path used to be. Next, mark north and south on your drawing, so you'll remember where the big shadows fall, and doodle in any really important details like "septic tank," "buried treasure" or "shark pool" that may make a difference to your design. No sense getting in a knot about scale here. Garden designs aren't based on how many squares on a grid have to be filled in, but on your materials and personal needs, and these will change. Just work on your concept of what will end up where; then put this map safely aside until later.

## Planning your garden's uses – a wish list

On a second sheet of paper, list things you would like to do in your garden (not only what you do now). If you want to stretch out in a hammock, be able to pick a bouquet to take to a friend, eat fresh salads from just outside your door, pick and dry some herbs, grow pumpkins for the kids or have some fresh snow peas for your stir-fry, write all this down. Put your head back and dream. Don't rush. Keep this list around for a few days to add to or change. Browse through some gardening magazines and books and make a note of the ornamental plants that catch your eye. Try to figure out what it is about the plant that you like — the variegated foliage? The big-leafed, tropical look? The big red flowers? Maybe a little pond would transform your life, or a secret garden hidden behind some foliage. Jot down all the things that tickle your fancy, whether they are immediately doable or not.

For many reasons, grand plans seem to die at this point, and this is why lists can be so useful. Review carefully how the following lists are made up, because they can be tailored to fit any task from building a house to changing the world.

## Creating an action list

Now, keeping one eye on your "wish" list, prepare a second list of what actions will need to take place to fulfill your garden dreams. Start a firm list of items you will need and beside each item note the required action.

**Visualize!**

Visualize your objective as clearly as possible during this process. Stretching out on a hammock will require a hammock — where will you get it? You will also need two suitably strong uprights, which could consist of any sturdy items that are 12 feet apart. A fence corner could be one end, and the clothesline pole could be the anchor point. Or you might have to anchor the uprights. This might require more questions: Who will you ask for help? How will you fasten the hammock to the uprights? How high must you hang the

### My action list

| ITEM | ACTION |
| --- | --- |
| Hammock | Find one – catalogues? Sporting-goods store? |
| Uprights | Check Bill's woodpile? Lumber store |
| | Phone Mary about recycling pile |
| Shovel | Find in shed. Phone Dad about how deep to make the hole |
| | for the post |
| Cement | Hardware store? Or look for leftover bag in Bill's basement |
| Rocks | Can dig out of veggie garden |

hammock so that your bum doesn't bump the ground? Get your creative juices flowing and think through every step from start to finish, identifying each item you need and how you will get it.

**Visualize some more**

Lie in your imaginary hammock (but don't fall asleep). How about those snow peas? They're really easy to grow, but they cost a fortune in the stores. Snow peas grow tall, so they'll need support of some kind. Old garden netting or fishnet is best. Do you have a source for any of this? Do you have a fence or carport to string the support against? You'll have to be able to reach the snow peas with the hose unless you care to hand-water. How will you attach the top of the netting? With hooks? Or should you string a rope through the top horizontally and tie it up high on each end? Where can you buy snow pea seeds? They probably have them at the corner nursery, and they are listed in all the veggie seed catalogues. You'll need to loosen a trench about a foot wide in the soil where the seeds are to go and scratch in a nice layer of compost, minus the big bits.

**Another action list**

| ITEM | ACTION |
| --- | --- |
| Pea seeds | Garden store, seed catalogues, seed swap? |
| | Ask Carol for some? |
| Piece of netting | Call Bill for advice on finding fishnet |
| | Price garden netting at plant nursery |
| Rope and hooks | Check shed, check closet, check Bill's shed |
| Water | Hose won't reach fence. Find bucket? |
| | Ask for watering can for birthday |

Now, how about that salad garden? You'll want something close to the house for this and not in the sunniest part of your yard, either. Most lush salad greens get quite limp when they're in direct sunlight with inadequate water, as you've found when you've left the grocery bag on the front porch while you've wandered off to visit a neighbour. What do you see outside your door now (and don't neglect your front-door area if the conditions are better)? Would it be an easy place to water? Is there enough room? Will you have to dig up grass, or cover it with cardboard and pile fresh compost or good soil on top to start a garden?

You can buy seeds easily and plant them early, because (as the packets will tell you) most greens like to be planted while it's cool out, but the seedlings won't show up for a bit. Therefore, you'll want to mark the new garden so that folks approaching such a well-travelled porthole, don't leave their bicycles and grocery bags on top of it before the seeds sprout. You can divide off new kitchen gardens with old bricks, driftwood, large painted rocks, planted-up rubber boots or whatever you have that will signal to another human that something is going on in there. Then you have to figure out what you want in your salads, but that's another chapter.

You can see how your lists will develop as you take the time to daydream about your garden and how it will look at certain times during its growth. Once you have visualized your needs properly, you can start sorting through your garage, hardware store flyers and neighbours' woodpiles for the necessary items. You may need a shovel to dig a hole and ... well, you get the drift.

## Back to your map!

Pick up your garden map again and start looking at it in conjunction with your fresh list of garden wants. Now you'll be able to mesh your wishes with a definite location and specific needs and requirements. For example, draw a circle showing how far your hose will reach from the tap, or how far you are willing to walk with a bucket. I recommend bringing your garden as close to your house as possible. You'll use it more, and you'll water and weed it more. Leave the outlying areas for such things as badminton-playing and hammock-lying (a very competitive sport, that).

## Choosing the plants

Start the list of plants that you want in your garden. The usual definitions are **edibles** and **ornamentals**. Of the ornamentals, you can choose by

**Incredible gardening tip**

Some of us never figure out why our neighbour, Bill, gets so much done in a day while we're still trying to remember how to get our pyjamas off. Well, Bill has a secret — he's methodical! He figures out what he needs to do, he makes a list and, by gum, *he sticks with it!* Bill has discovered that sheer tenacity and the sense of order that a piece of paper brings can make all the difference to a day. And he still has the rest of the week left! Bill's tip would be to *actually use these lists!*

physical dimension (I want a tall, thin shrub to hide the drainpipe. I want a low bush to screen the alien landing pad the people next door just built) or by a need to enhance your world (I need *red* flowers to match the door! And yellow over there so I can see flowers when I wash the dishes). You might want some scented plants, and some that attract butterflies or hummingbirds.

As for the edibles, start with what you really like to eat. It helps to cruise through a seed catalogue or recipe book for this part. Don't discount a vegetable because your kids won't eat it. Think of tasty berries and fresh greens with salad dressing, as well as the more obvious peas and tomatoes.

I strongly suggest that the new gardener who is considering planting annual veggies should stick to the simpler items listed in chapter 4 — those that don't need any special treatment to fulfill their life cycles. Experiment if you will, but if you are truly faint of heart, stay with some basics for the first year and add to your list of successes season by season.

## A CHECKLIST OF TOOLS

### Some handy ones (because that is all I own)

**Shovels and spades**

Someone once said that I was truly a woman who called a spade a spade, but I didn't know what one was at the time. Now that I own a spade, I do know the difference and I am a shovel-lover no more. Next time you have money to invest, go to your garden centre and say, "Charles, please lead me to your finest garden spade." Spades have a very narrow blade and are usually short-handled. Pick out one with a nice solid feel to it. Make sure the blade feels good and sturdy and that you can't twist it at all. Look at the price tag. Feel your eyes bug out in surprise. The little dickenses don't come cheap, but whatever you do, whenever possible, buy this tool. Protect it. Baby it. Clean it and oil it. You will never go back to a shovel again. You see, where a shovel will certainly work in soft soil, a spade will cut down right into the most horrible gravelly stuff, without all the grunting and heaving required to use a shovel. You can cut close to bushes, because you can direct your leg's energy right where you want it. You can dig postholes, tree holes and bulb holes with them. Save your broad old shovel for soil that's already broken up. I used to think I was just a weakling, but now I know that a woman is only as good as her shovel. Er, spade.

### Rakes

There are two kinds, the bamboo grass rake and the good old metal garden rake. We'll discuss the garden rake here. I use mine for slowly sifting the bigger gunk out of a new garden bed, for gathering rocks into a pile, and for pulling clumps of weeds toward me. Rakes are excellent for levelling and flattening an area after you have dug out the weeds. Their tines will catch on all the small twigs in the soil, too, so that you can brush them off into the compost heap. Sometimes I drop my rake down at an angle onto a clump of stubborn weeds to break it up and yank it out, rather than going to look for my shovel.

I use the handle of my rake to make a straight line in the soil when I want to plant a row of seeds, then I gently rake the soil over the little ditch I have made. Sometimes I gently rake my big old honeysuckle vine in the spring to loosen all the old leaves. I use my rake to hook tree branches down to where I can reach them to clip them or pick fruit, or I just tease off the fruit with the rake tines and try to catch them!

Rakes are also handy, used flat edge down, to pull the snow off of a too-laden greenhouse. You can lift young birds out of the pond (although the bamboo rake is better for this) or, heck, clean out a whole small pond by dredging it with a metal rake. Just be careful not to hurt the salamanders.

### Trowels

These are tiny shovels built for lifting small plants out of the soil, mixing potting soils (but hands are better), digging out young weeds or making small holes for bulbs. They are just right for putting in nursery plants and vegetable starts, because the

### The queen of spades

I have another use for my spade – I use its blade to cut through bramble vines. I just push the branches to the ground, hold them down with one foot and plunge the blade into them with a fearsome yell. Saves running into the house for the clippers!

hole is the right size. Like all tools, trowels should be built of stern stuff or the metal will simply bend under a good twist of the wrist.

### "Prongers"

Okay, I don't even know what these are really called, but they are as handy as all get-out. They have a sturdy handle and several inches of nice, solid, pencil-thin shaft, ending in two ... prongs. I have a few of these scattered around the yard. I ease out dandelions with them, loosen raspberry roots from the footpaths, follow and unearth tiny rootlets on a valuable plant, and otherwise prong out tightly wedged plants from impossible spots like paths or rock walls, with a minimum of root damage. I can reach into a matted root ball and gently separate a young specimen who does not belong there, or tease compressed plants into individual units for transplanting. If only I knew what it was called ...

### Hoses and nozzles

A good garden has hoses all over the darn place, because you never know when you'll need one. The hose should have a good spray nozzle, so that you don't freeze your thumb off trying to project a jet of water to hit that back dry area. Some say that the expensive spray nozzles are best, with their large selection of watering combinations (Mist? Jet? Drizzle?), but a truck ran over mine. The remaining stump is still quite sensitive to thumb pressure and gives an even, adjustable spray — perhaps even better than in its past life.

Hose nozzles normally have a piece of wire you can press under the back of the head to keep the water flowing while you release and rest your exhausted thumb. This is handy. You can nestle the nozzle into a crook of tree branch, direct it at the nearest garden corner and walk away, muttering, "I'm watering my garden!"

### Sprinklers and such

Although certain laws of nature say it is not possible, the world seems to be running out of water. In the midst of this thought, I note that here we are with our crazy sprinklers, watering the paths,

**Hosiery department**

My favourite hose accoutrements are the little metal "Y"s that screw into the tap so that you can have a hose running, and at the same time fill a bucket to dilute some manure tea. Is life not bliss?

sidewalks … *the air* for God's sake! We're sprinkling the *air!* My little rant aside, please do consider the planet and buy a soaker hose or some other irrigation system that will deliver water to exactly where you want it. When you have the soil nice and moist, put another layer of mulch on it to keep the moisture there. And if you're sprinkling a lawn, think of letting it get a bit long and watering it much less, if at all.

## Tools I personally don't use, but just to be a completist …

### Forks

The garden variety of these, of course, look like giant dinner forks with very long tines. You can use them for turning and loosening newly broken soil, turning compost, mixing in manure, throwing hay, and protecting your family from predators in B movies. They are excellent for gathering root crops because the chances of actually piercing a potato or beet are marginally reduced. The four-pronged version with the thicker tines is a pitchfork or garden fork. The five-pronged one, with thinner, longer tines, is technically a manure fork (and the best fork for keeping the alien invaders at bay).

### Hoes

Those raised with a hoe in hand gape in amazement at those without. I've never used one, but I can tell you this much: Hoes are flat blades on long handles, the idea being to pull the blade across young weeds, thereby ripping their tiny heads off and leaving them defenceless in the sun. Is that right? Call me if I'm wrong.

## GETTING MUD ON YOUR SHOES

Although spring is considered the best time to start putting in a garden, you can begin building your garden areas at any time of the year, and can actually plant an interesting array of horticultural wonders during each season.

## Choosing a site

Your obvious first step is to choose a site at which to start digging. The minimum number of tools you'll need is one, the lowly shovel, although adding a pitchfork or rake to this will do absolutely no harm. Pruning shears will come in handy if you have to cut away any brambles. A tarp or large piece of cardboard is good to have around as well.

Suitably armed, view your first growing area. Lift away any obviously unnecessary items such as chunks of wood, big rocks, bicycles and old refrigerators. Put these items aside in case you can incorporate them into your plan later.

If you get an experienced gardener to come by now, she can tell you if any of the unrecognizable bits growing in your garden-to-be are actually valuable plants, so that you can move them out of harm's reach. It's a good idea to tag these plants as well, because new gardeners frequently forget plant names.

## Preparing the soil

Now that you've chosen your site, rip out any remaining undesirable brambles and weeds. To do this, get the shovel under the place where the stem hits the ground. Push it under as far as you can and lever the plant out of the dirt. Use the shovel to bash as much soil off the root ball as you can, because this is good stuff and you want it in the garden. Toss the now bare-rooted weed onto the tarp. You see, if you put it right into the compost heap it may not die but re-root and flower; if you leave it out in the sun to cook for a couple of days, it will be as dead as a doornail and safe to compost. As you dig under each type of weed you will see how its roots grow. Dandelions have a deep taproot and you'll have to be careful to get the whole thing out, so dig deep. Buttercups have a flat clump of root, so if you put the shovel in far enough away from where the stem leaves the soil, you can easily get the whole root. Start learning who has what underneath. You'll come across rocks, too; toss them in a pile to the side. They can come in handy to mark edges or divide sections. Cleaning the soil like this is the toughest part of the whole thing, but keep heart and do it right. The harder you work now, the easier your job will be later.

When you are satisfied that all the big roots and rocks have been removed, you can use your shovel tip or fork to break up chunks of soil. Loosen hard crusts by heaving up a clump and bashing it with the back of the shovel head until it falls apart. You're trying to make a consistency in which little rootlets would like to grow. Try not to stand in the middle of your garden to do this work, as you'll just keep compacting the soil. Stand to the side and keep breaking up the soil in a row as you walk. Long thin beds are preferable to blocks for this reason.

## Making your bed (but not lying in it!)

In the olden days, gardeners dug down to put in a garden; these days, many gardeners build up, by creating a mound or by actually building a raised edge with wood, cement blocks or bricks.

Here's why (whew, you needed a break about now, anyway).

A raised bed doesn't get walked on as a flat garden does, because you can build it so that you can reach into the middle without stepping into the bed. In this way the soil stays loose. Loose soil doesn't need tilling — a quick re-digging each spring should do it. Therefore, there's air in the soil for plants and bugs and the water can drain from it easily. A raised bed also heats up better in the spring. Because the planting area is more permanent than the ever-changing paths and rows of a flat garden, the fertilizing agents you apply feed the growing area, not next year's path. Water, too, can be applied to just the growing area.

If you are putting in a mound garden without edging, just dig and loosen the soil in the space you want to use. As you loosen it, it will fluff up above the level of the ground, and you can increase this effect by digging a drain trench around the perimeter and adding that soil to your

**Raised beds**

To start a raised bed, keep piling that loose soil in the middle as you break it up. Then, having picked your material for the edges (old cement blocks, old cedar fencing or driftwood), dig a perimeter trench a few inches deep and as wide as your edging material.

17

mound. Rake this flat on the top, and stand back and admire your first planting area.

Throw the soil from the trench into the centre of the bed. Apply your edging material in any way imaginable and use nails, screws and old baling wire to hold it in place. Fill spaces on the outer edge with your rock collection to hold up loose boards, then kick the dirt back against it on the inside and stamp as hard as you can, all the way along. (The more financially secure can bypass all this mess by hiring a crew and watching nervously from the kitchen window.) Now reach over with your rake and pull the soil down so it lies flat in the bed, and keep tugging out those remaining roots and rocks. The soil will be higher than the surrounding ground and you can add compost or other fill at this point.

It's good to put these beds in early, cover the soil with good stuff like compost, hay, leaves or manure and let it sit a while — a week, a month, a year. It can only get better and better in there as the mulch on top breaks down.

## Planting

To plant your garden, just pull the mulch back and clean up the surface area by pulling out any stubborn weeds. Rake it flat again, remove pebbles and such, use your shovel handle to put in rows or holes, and plant those seeds! Although there is a marvellous thing called broadcast seeding, which involves scattering seed willy-nilly, marked rows will pay off for the new gardener because it can take years to be able to identify each new plant as it comes up, and the weed seeds will be sprouting about now, too. If something comes up in a straight line it gives you a fighting chance to accurately decide who needs yanking out.

## Timing is everything

Although your garden can be put in at any time of year, certain seeds should be planted only at certain times, depending on the temperature they need to germinate and whether they grow best in cold or hot seasons. This is determined by where on the planet they spent their first few thousand years: northern Europe? The Amazon? Learning where a plant was developed from the wild state will tell you when to sow the seed, but the brief guide that follows will save you a lot of time and energy.

### Cool spring planting

The basic definition of cool spring or "early" planting is working with the soil without its being a sodden pile of muck, and without your feeling unpleasantly cool while working. Lettuce and most other salad greens can go in quite early in the year, as can broccoli, cabbage, asparagus, beets, carrots, onions, peas, radishes, spinach, Chinese greens such as bok choy and gai lan, and potatoes. This is also a good time of year to stick in perennial plants such as raspberries, sorrel, rhubarb and all the kitchen herbs except basil.

### Warm early summer planting

The rule of thumb for warm planting is that if you could sit on the soil on your bare bum, without shivering or making a face, the ground is warm enough to plant the following veggies — beans, celery, corn, cucumber, squashes, tomatoes, sunflowers, tomatillos, eggplants and peppers. It's not too late to plant perennials such as berry bushes, but make sure that you shade them for a few days, and water them well for a couple of weeks.

### Fall plantings

When the leaves fall, it's time for fall planting — why do you think they call it fall? Garlic and onions, leek sets and young perennial broccoli are all good experiments for your garden. Since we've seen potatoes come up by themselves in the spring, we know that we can try sticking some out under a healthy layer of mulch in late fall. Even peas, if you plant them six inches deep, will fight their way up before you've planted your spring seeds. Some of us have seen tomato plants growing in our compost heaps before we see our garden seedlings in spring, but remember that the heap gives off some heat from the process of decomposition, which the garden bed does not. Fall, since it does not strain plants with excessive heat and dryness, is a good time to put in perennial plants like berries, trees and herbs.

Now, get all that mud off your shoes!

# JUST THE ESSENTIALS

3

"Most soil analysts see great significance in electrical charged particles or ions, cations and anions. They examine how the bulk of plant nutrients are taken up by electrically charged chemical elements which are either cations (positive ions) or anions (negatively charged ions). Cation Exchange in the soil is a complicated study in itself revolving around the analysis of the ions of different chemicals and also the significance of pH. As opposed to the above, some organic researchers have given lectures and slide presentations to illustrate that even large particles are absorbed by plant roots and made available to plants without cation exchange."

— anonymous Sunshine Coast soil expert

Whew! My only concern was whether or not to water the garden the next day, and then I read the above bit of garden lore and my world turned upside down. I tossed and turned all night in my bed. Do I have enough cations to balance my anions? If not, how can I get more of those cations, anyway? Are my ions doing whatever they do to my pH? Are all of my particles adequately charged? Should I be doing something? *Arrgghh!* And how did growing a pea get so complicated? Fortunately, when I awoke in the morning and looked out the window I realized it had all been just a bad dream. There was my garden, and my little row of peas, and they still wanted the same humble things I did. Air. Water. Food. Light. Okay, I also wanted a trip to the Azores, but that was beside the point.

## A SIMPLER VIEW ...

All you really need to have are the fab four: air, water, food and light.

### Air

This item is such an easy element to get hold of that you can just about take it off your list, which leaves only three elements to worry about. Isn't gardening easy? One thing you may want to be concerned with is how clean the air is around your food plants. This is only a concern if your garden is near your driveway or along the side of a road, where exhaust fumes might be inadvertently blown onto your dainty veggies, loading them with nasty toxins. If this is the case, either install some type of fence or dig up some shrub plants of a type you will not be eating and plant them in a row to separate the road from the garden. Another option is to plant your inedibles near the cars and move your veggies farther back. It's hard to make a rule about how far from the vehicles the garden should be, but "as far as you can" is a good start, especially without a band of plants to act as a living air filter.

People often forget that air is necessary for plant roots. Keeping your soil loose by turning and digging the soil well before you plant will help with this, and you can assist by not compacting it by walking on it. Some folks put down old boards to walk on in the garden. I have placed some flat rocks so that I can step onto them to weed or pick.

## Water

Another cinch. However, there are some things to learn about using water. For one, plants can't walk over and turn on the tap, so humans must deliver water to them when it doesn't rain. Baby roots reach only a little way into the top of the soil, and when that soil dries out, the seedlings die quickly.

### Encouraging deep roots

As they mature, plant roots will reach many feet down to the constantly damp portions of the soil. Encourage the roots to dive down to the damp layer (rather than up to the surface for a few drops of water) by watering your garden *thoroughly*. Water early in the morning if you can, so that plant leaves have a chance to dry out during the day.

### Mulch

To keep all that precious water from evaporating back up into the cosmos, cover the soil surface around the plants with a mulch of old hay, compost, cardboard, sawdust, yard clippings or whatever, deep enough to keep the soil shaded. With watering restrictions becoming more prevalent, mulching makes even more sense, as it will reduce the amount of water you use and keep the soil cooler to boot. It also will keep soil moisture more consistent and the plant roots won't suffer stress. More on this later!

To tell if you need to water, pull the mulch back from beside a plant and stick your finger down a couple of inches. If your soil feels dry and hot, water it, and take as much time as you can afford to do it well, so that you don't have to do

### Room for worms

Air is a good thing to have in your soil, as you can see, but it's hard to force it down there should you want to add some to your garden. An easy way to introduce miles of tiny airways to your soil is to encourage worms to do all the work for you. You'll notice worms love your compost heap – that is because it's full of the half-decomposed plant matter they live on. If you dig that compost into your soil, and add a mulch of straw or leaves to draw worms up to the moist, cool, protected surface for another snack, you can keep those busy little critters working for you. And not only will they constantly burrow about, making tunnels, they will also line those little paths with worm castings, for which, by the way, some people pay good money. So be good to your worms, and they'll be good to you.

it as often. One test for good watering is to go back in an hour and feel the soil again. Loosen some soil to about four inches deep to make sure water has seeped down that far.

**Midsummer syndrome: plan now for the coming doldrums**

A common syndrome among new gardeners is the loss of interest about mid-summer, just when watering becomes crucial. Plan your garden according to this human frailty! Ask for a hose for your birthday (go on, tell me to get a life) or do anything else you have to do to end up with a hose you can leave out all summer, just for your veggies. This will reduce your resistance to unscrewing the lawn sprinkler or whatever. Make sure you have a clear path from your door to the water valve, so that you don't put off running out to turn the hose on because you have to leap lawn chairs and dog bowls, and pull little Annie's bike out of the way.

**Too much water**

Some people will notice that in times of heavy rain water will pool in their veggie gardens. This can mean that the soil is too compacted, and that the earth layer underneath is not porous enough to percolate the water through. Perhaps there is heavy clay or rock under there. To cure this, you may have to move the garden to a slight slope where the water can run off naturally, or build up raised boxes so that the soil can drain to lower levels quickly. If the soil is dense (like clay) you might have to dig in random amounts of sand and compost to create tiny air pockets within it, which will hold air and help it drain.

# Food

This is where most humans run into problems, and they tend to project all their own food issues onto their plants. Binge or purge? Feast or famine? This is another area where a little information is all you need to make good decisions. But first, take a detour to the sidebar on the following page that describes the "forest model" — how the forest manages to feed and balance itself without (sometimes in spite of) the meddling influence of humans.

### The forest model

The way we garden today is very different from when we picked what was available from the forest edge. Some say we did a lot less damage when we harvested from the forest, and people are madly searching for ways to integrate our methods of gardening with a more natural, low-maintenance and sustainable style.

Visit a forest, or simply visualize one. How is this different from your garden? Okay, besides the 120-foot trees. Okay, and besides the mountain. And the glacier. And the rutting elk. I mean, how is it *really* different?

First, look down. See any bare earth? Nope. It's all sealed away under layers of moss, rotting leaves and broken twigs. There are worms right under the surface, eating all the decomposing bits and making air tunnels, and leaving fertile droppings. If you look up a bit, you'll notice young plants growing amongst the old, and that the very old, when they finally topple, end up breaking down and re-feeding the young ones. They also leave a circle of space that offers a source of high, diffused light. Most of the young plants don't have to start out in harsh sunlight.

You'll notice the feeling of moisture around you. Plants like the high humidity that occurs when they grow closely together, and where the sun can't bake the soil dry.

You'll hear a variety of bird calls, and if you pick the moss away from a tree branch you'll see various little bugs and worms working away.

You'll notice that a large variety of plants are growing in a small space, that berry bushes push in under the large trees, and that ferns grow under that, and careful analysis of the moss and duff will show lots of dainty little plants spread about. You'll see that different plants push themselves out around the forest edges into the sunlight.

Here's what you won't see — a human standing around with a hose and a box of fertilizer. No one is there to prune the trees into a "balanced" canopy. They grow evenly by themselves. And is the forest a neglected, high-care, bug-eaten mess? No way! This whole machine runs without human interference, and runs hugely and abundantly.

How can we relate the forest model to our own yards, without straining our minds? We know that the forest always has layers of nutrients breaking down in it, so we know it will help our plants to have compost and leaves crumbling nicely nearby. We'll find out how to do this easily in the section on nourishment. We know that huge trees can grow very well merely by eating (through their roots) their own fallen leaves and rotting branches, and by coexisting nicely with the surrounding plants. We can then draw a parallel with our gardens and realize that if we offer back the waste leaves of our own plants, these will contain the elements the plants need most.

For example, imagine that patch of lilies back there by the gate, the clump that grows so prolifically with no help from you or me. That patch has been feeding off its own rotting leaves for the past million years, so why would we think that it actually needs some stuff out of a little box? Keeping this in mind, you'll realize the importance of a composting system, wherein everything you pull *out* of the garden bed for your own convenience now (thinnings, damaged leaves, weeds) is *replaced* at some point for the plants to eat next year, or you'll just be stealing everybody's dinner! What is missing from this equation is the part of the plant that we don't put back — the part we eat. But many people on the planet apply their own waste to the soil so that, in fact, almost all the matter and most of the bulk is returned to the garden and no elements are missing at all. Culturally, we in the West are not all attuned to this concept, so we might want to add some extras to the compost heap to make up for the missing "fecal fraction."

### Compost's the most!

Compost on its own is a pretty complete food. You cannot use too much of it, it's free, it encourages worms to come to your garden, and it leaves space at the landfills for all those stupid little boxes. Compost is a slow-release food that will end the feast/famine problems of nitrogen fertilizers. Compost contains things like sulfur and copper that our gardens need, and that the conventional fertilizers from the garden store do not supply. Compost can be thrown in a pile in any old corner of the yard and is made up of scrap material in your yard such as weed clumps, prunings, dead flower heads and lawn clippings, as well as waste matter from the kitchen, including all vegetable matter (from carrot tops to squash

husks), eggshells, coffee and tea grounds and undyed hair clippings. If this were all you fed your garden, it would likely be a happy place. If you added to your compost the occasional bag of manure from your latest visit to the country, the leaves from your trees, and some wood ash from a neighbour with a wood stove, your garden would be offered just about all the major ingredients it could possibly need, and would be ecstatic. This sounds too easy, but it is the exact formula used in healthy gardens for the past few thousand years — if not longer.

### Free fertilizer

As with the various vitamin families such as A, B and C, certain plant nutrients are given food values. Some of the most common, and necessary, are **N: nitrogen, P: phosphorus, K: potassium, S: sulfur, Ca: calcium**. People often ask how to get these great letters for their own yards without spending a lot of money and bringing in the use of a large factory, so here is a big surprise for you.

## "Ask Astilbe"

**Q:** Astilbe, how come all my *good, expensive* plant books worry so much about pH, and you haven't even discussed it yet. Huh?

**A:** Now that we have uncomplicated the topic of plant food, let's briefly (I said briefly) consider the topic of pH (from *potenz*, German for power, and H, the symbol for hydrogen). There is a huge amount of talk about pH, and whether it should be 6.3 or, in fact, 5.8 for a particular plant. It becomes a pretty crazy concept when you consider how hard it is to tell what your soil pH level is in each square foot (because it will change depending on whether an old cedar tree stood there, or a burn pile is under your new garden) and in what area it changes by how much, let alone how much *exactly* you have to add to change it, and how long that change will take. But your naggy neighbour, Bill, will swear that nothing can grow well in your garden without constant monitoring of the pH. What gives? Worry not! The experts down at the Rodale Experimental Farms in Kutztown, Pennsylvania rediscovered that if good compost is continuously added to any garden soil, it will slowly bring it to a state that is agreeable to a wide range of plants. Most West Coasters can assume that their soil is acidic and should dust a light layer of wood ash or dolomite lime over their gardens several times a year, which will help it become more neutral.

The weeds in your garden are much higher in those nutrients than anything you can buy in the store. That's why you've been encouraged to use them in teas and as mulch.

Below is a chart to show you how nutrient-rich some weeds are, and just how powerful the planet already was before fertilizer packagers came along.

### Nutrients in organic matter

| ORGANIC MATTER | NUTRIENTS: POUNDS PER TON OF MATERIAL | | | | |
| --- | --- | --- | --- | --- | --- |
| | N | P | K | S | Ca |
| Canada thistle | 54 | 13 | 82 | – | 76 |
| Chickweed | 77 | 34 | 220 | – | 28 |
| Crab grass | 38 | 18 | 93 | – | – |
| Morning glory | 72 | 19 | 94 | – | 27 |
| Bone meal | 60 | 400 | 10 | – | – |
| Cow manure | 11 | 3 | 9 | .9 | 6 |
| Ground seaweed | 20 | 4 | 40 | – | – |
| Straw (average, non-legume) | 17 | 5 | 26 | 3 | 13 |
| Wood ash | – | 32 | 106 | – | – |

## Light

Light pours down out of the sky and generally hits the planet pretty well head-on, so there are no real worries here for the home gardener. Being human, however, and full of endless anxieties, we sometimes figure our plants are getting a bit too much light or a bit too little.

**Too much light**
You know you have too much light if you transplant little seedlings into a new row and they promptly flop over on the dirt like Raggedy Ann dolls. They just didn't have enough time to get their water-sucking functions back in order before that old sun fried their stuffings. A cure for this is to transplant during light rain (or at least on cloudy days) or, if you can't wait for rain, to water gently and then pull some tufts of long grass from along the fence and build little huts around your transplants. You can also lay bracken ferns on top of them (they will wither just as the plant takes hold)

or shake hay bits loosely over them, just enough to keep the soil around them looking shaded.

Sometimes we think there is too much light when, in fact, there is too little water. This is a common problem in container gardens, which, depending on the size of the pot, usually cannot possibly keep too much water from evaporating during the day. You can help by mulching the surface with moss, sawdust or pebbles, leaving a couple of free inches at the top of the pot for generous watering, and moving the pots to a partly shaded spot.

Another example of the light/water combo going askew is when we leave a flat of seedlings just inside a window, and the sun comes out and cooks them thoroughly before we can get home from work. (I have tried to use this as an excuse to leave early, but my boss just doesn't get the enormous implications.) If you suspect the sun will broil your little beauties, tape a sheet of newspaper over the window glass where the sun will be hitting it. The diffused light will be much better for your plants, and the paper will come down easily when you're ready to put the "kids" outside.

## Too little light

As an outdoor problem, this generally means that trees or buildings are blocking the sun in your growing area, which may at first seem an incurable problem. But crafty old gardeners have found various ways to manipulate their environment to get the most out of it. Here are some of the most popular courses to take, rather than having the house to the south of you taken down to one storey to save your precious tomatoes.

First of all, analyze what actually is in the brighter portions of your yard and figure out which items are portable. Move non-living things like compost heaps and garden sheds into the shade, if this will free some room in the sun. Next, make sure you're using your sunny areas to the maximum by vertical gardening up walls and fences.

Decide which of your plants actually need all that light in your only sunny bit, and move all the ones that will tolerate more shade. Look at chapter 12 on growing in the shade to see what will

**More trees!**

With the ozone thinning as it is, some folks are complaining that certain of their plants look sunburned. This is a good excuse to start planting more trees in our yards to offer some shade during the height of summer for years to come. Plant now. In five years, you'll be glad you did.

tolerate the dark. Move your main growing area (usually your annuals such as squash, beans and tomatoes) into the brightest spot. Read chapter 7 on edible landscaping to get ideas on incorporating your sun-loving plants into a better site, reserving your sheltered areas for more shade-tolerant plants such as raspberries, rhubarb and lettuce. Maximize the light you do have by covering your walkways and areas around beds with sawdust, white gravel or hay. This will reflect an amazing amount of light back toward the plants.

# EASY VEGGIES AND
# HOW TO GROW THEM

4

## BRAVE VEGETABLES FOR THE
## FAINT OF HEART

As good teachers know, if neophytes are given
projects that they can complete successfully they'll
be more interested in and excited about trying
something more challenging next time. This is a
list of veggies that will give the beginner something to crow about. They are resilient, recognizable and easy to start. Do you see cauliflower
here? Okra? Celery? Nooooooo!

## Beans

Like peas, beans come in varieties with edible portions that are either just the seeds (such as fava or chickpeas) or the whole pods (such as green bush beans), but you can always eat the whole pods of any type if you pick them small enough. Taste them often to see how you like them! Beans are good to eat right off the plant in small quantities. There are short "bush" varieties you should watch for because they don't need support and generally are very good producers. Check your seed packet to see whether you are planting "pole" beans, which will need something to climb, or "bush," which are tidy little things that don't get very big but may still fall over just to bug you. Beans are pretty hard to kill, unless they get really dry. Like peas, bean seeds can get a head start if you soak them overnight, but skip that if your soil is moist and soft. Beans are unlike peas in that they are not cold-weather plants, so don't plant them until the soil feels warm when you place your hand on it. This is usually around May. Beans don't mind a bit of compost in the soil, but for some reason I have never given mine a midsummer feed and they have given me lots of beans anyway.

### Pole bean vs. bush bean – what gives?

In a few years you will laugh about the day you confused a "pole" and a "bush" bean, or didn't know why the difference was important. The fact is that some beans are genetically programmed to grow very big and long, and to twine their way up supports into the sun (pole beans), and some are programmed to grow into tidy little bushes. Catalogues clearly label these two so that you can make an informed decision about your purchase, depending on your space limitations. If you have lots of lateral space, and can hang string or netting, the climbing or "pole" beans will use your space well, but if you have nowhere to hang netting, and don't have any pole material, try some nice little bush beans. Within the pole group and the bush group there are a wide variety of flavours and colours to choose from, all nice to experiment with, so go ahead and do so. Although the pole varieties seem more vigorous and can actually become quite huge, you can get a nice haul off your little bushes, and they are easier to tuck into garden beds where space is tight.

## Garlic

Garlic cloves, like most snowboarders, need a good stretch of cold weather to make them happy in spring. It is best to plant them in late October or early November, but they will certainly live through everything from early October to early March. They prefer a healthy soil full of compost and, unlike potatoes (or snowboarders, for that matter), like a good shaking of wood ash or lime added a couple of times through the winter and spring. Organic garlic is best to plant because you know it hasn't been treated with a chemical that keeps it from sprouting, as some of the cloves you'd find in a grocery store have been. Very disappointing, that!

Hold the head of garlic in your hand and break off the individual cloves. Try not to break off too much of their little papery coats, as they protect them from rotting. Look at the cloves closely and you will see a pointy end and a flatter end. The flat end grows the roots and should go toward the bottom of the hole. If you want a good experiment, put a garlic clove in a dish of water for a few days. You'll easily see where the roots are starting from, and will never be confused again.

Take your handful of clove sections out to your garden, and soften the top few inches of your chosen patch with a shovel or rake. Push the cloves into the soil, anywhere from one inch below the surface to just protruding from it. Throw on any mulching material you have. The garlic may start growing before the cold weather hits, but will die down for winter. In early spring you will see your garlic coming up. It is optional to top-dress or add manure tea to your garlic, but you will certainly get a better haul of bigger heads if you treat it well by feeding it through the spring and by watering it now and then.

## Peas

Peas and beans are great things to plant, because they are nutritious, good for the soil, and come in a large variety of types. There are all sorts of peas

— ones just for peas and ones just for pods, and some good for both. The package will tell you whether they will need support or not. The thing about peas is that even with some pretty heavy neglect you are bound to get a few sweet, tender peas on your vines, and that will be all the encouragement you'll need to spend a little more attention on them next year. Keep them watered, and keep picking off all the pods. Like beans, peas just want to produce seed, and if you keep thwarting that need by picking the pods before they mature, they'll just keep making more to keep up.

You can plant peas early in the spring. Just soak the seed overnight, and push them into the soil between one-half and two inches deep — honest! Some of my gardening books say that pea soil needs no special treatment, but I have better luck when I dig some compost into the trench as I'm planting and give the plants some manure tea when they start to put out flowers (or before, or later, if you missed!).

**Warning!**

Since peas and early greens are the first real edibles to come up in the spring, all the hungry critters such as slugs and snails will be just as eager as you are to see them! You'll need some tricks to keep your seedlings safe. You can leave some weeds around, either pulled or growing, so the that slugs have something else to eat. Remember that in a well-cleaned garden there is *nothing* to eat except your seedlings — compulsive weeders, take note! Keep mulch pulled away from seedlings. Set traps, such as material from your compost bucket placed on some cardboard, and when the critters come a-munching pick them up and dispose of them in any manner compliant with your religious beliefs. You might want to start your baiting earlier than you plant, to get a head start. And remember — slugs are nocturnal, so keep a flashlight by the door with your boots so it'll be easy to rush out there and be a warrior at the right time.

## Onions

Onion sets are cheap to buy and fun to stick into the ground and watch. Do mix some wood ash into the soil for onions, wait for a good rain, and then plant the little "sets" (baby onions) in the dirt up to their shoulders (some say "waists," some say "necks"). They like bright sun. You will have to weed around them, but hey! When the tops die down, you'll be pulling up slightly bigger onions or, if they were particularly happy, *really* big onions. You can leave these in the sun for the day (or two if it's dry), then dust off the dirt and bring them in. Stored one layer deep in a dry spot, they'll keep for a long time.

Many say it is not worth growing onions because they're so cheap in the store, but people who have mastered onions tend to move on to the onion's exotic cousins — leeks and shallots! So add them to your first-year list for confidence-building. An added advantage for those who run out of onions all the time is your newfound ability to run out and pick one when you need one, because you can eat them at any size.

## Potatoes

I talk a lot about potatoes because they are an easy, healthy and affordable food source. Although proper soil preparation and hilling will certainly increase your yield, potatoes will give you some return even if you just lay them on the ground and kick some dirt over them. Another great attraction is their power to break up ground for next year's garden, so start with these if you have picked out a site already. You can plant the sprouted potatoes that are in your cupboard, or buy organic potatoes from the store. If you'd like to give the potatoes a hand, break up the surface soil a bit with a shovel or pitchfork and lay the potatoes in the softened area, about one foot apart, then cover them up, a little or a lot — just make it dark down there. Spend the summer throwing tasty bits like leaves and straw at them, or yard prunings and dried weed clumps, and let them grow through that. Potatoes do need semi-decent watering, so plunge the hose through that mess if it gets really dry and give them a good splash. When the tops start to yellow and die (and different varieties of potatoes die off at different times), pull back the mulch, dig around the base of the potato stem, and start pulling out dinner! You can actually harvest the little potatoes at any

### Perpetual potatoes

Fall harvest of potatoes is a satisfying pastime that will quickly fill your food basket. But don't dig potatoes until you need them – they'll last just fine under the soil and mulch. The ones you miss will pop up in the spring as new plants, which leads to my friend Peter's perpetual potato patch. He adds a new layer of mulch to his potatoes each spring and pulls out the big ones each fall. He's had the patch for 10 years now.

time of year by reaching under the mulch and soil and pulling them off the root but, like babies, they put on a lot of weight in the last month, so hold off if high pound production is your aim.

**Some more techniques**

A friend's father phoned her and asked her the best way to plant potatoes. She told him to plant them in hills. He phoned weeks later to complain about her suggestion, and she went to visit his garden to see what was wrong. What was wrong was that he had built nice hills out of soil, and had planted the potatoes in the top. As they sprouted greens, they fell over.

Go to your cupboard and take a good look at a potato. It will have small dents (called "eyes") scattered over it. These are the little pockets where the green growth will appear if you plant the spud. You can plant a whole potato, but you will get a bigger patch if you cut it into pieces (each piece including an eye). The bigger the piece, the bigger the resulting plant, so don't be too stingy. Dip each cut piece into wood ash or let it dry for three or four days before planting. This will keep it from rotting.

If you want to plant a potato that already has some growth at the eyes, plant it so that the most growth is pointing upward, to reduce the length of time it will take to break ground. Don't worry too much about this — if you planted it the wrong way round, it will grow out of the bottom, around the sides, and up to the sky. It will just take a little longer, that's all. Once a potato has established a healthy top, it will start putting out roots, and the new potatoes will develop along the roots. If soil is "hilled" up the stem of the plant, it will produce roots from the stem that grow into the soil, and will grow some more potatoes from those roots, as well. Generally, the mother potato will then weaken and shrivel (and will never let her little spuds forget it).

How deeply you plant a potato is not crucial. A potato left almost uncovered on the ground will turn green and put out some new growth, but you won't get much in the way of new roots and potatoes. A potato that is planted a foot deep in heavy clay soil will tucker itself out trying to get a stem up to the soil surface and it won't have much poop left for "baby" production, either. But any hole between three and six inches deep will grow you some extra potatoes. Potatoes will be happier in a healthy, loose, brown soil, but will survive under almost any condition. They will just not give you as much.

A less space-hungry method of potato farming is the tire tower. Stack two vehicle tires and fill the centre with soil. Plant a couple of potatoes — you can grow Jerusalem artichokes this way as well — in the top one, under a few inches of soil. When the potatoes are about a foot tall, put another tire on top and fill it with soil. Do this again as the plant grows. Keep the tire tower watered. In the fall, lift the towers off, knock the soil into buckets for another project and collect your potatoes. This works well in cramped spaces or where your new garden is full of old tires.

## Radishes

Root crops are hard for a first-year garden because new gardens are usually still full of rocks and sticks — things that fibrous roots can just work around, but that can cause big-rooted vegetables such as carrots and beets to get twisted. Radishes are small enough to grow between the rocks and are satisfying to plant because they mature so fast. Just keep thinning them by pulling out the smallest of two growing too closely together and sooner or later you'll pull out an honest-to-gosh radish.

## Squashes

There are lots of picky instructions for planting squashes, but for all the fussing it will end up best if you just learn from the one growing from last year's seed in the compost heap. Hmm, it's moist and warm in there, and full of rich food. Why plant squashes in the garden at all? They may not produce much for you if they're too cold or dry, but given compost-heap conditions, you'll get lots of healthy vines that will produce oohs and aahs.

**Warning!**

Never eat any green part of a potato plant, even the potato itself. It is poisonous to your system. Cut away the green parts with a knife and eat the rest.

**Eww! Mildew!**

Squash, including zukes, exhibit a powdery, mildewy condition (called "powdery mildew," for some reason) late in the season. Snap off those leaves as they appear. But don't worry about the plant. This mildew, like lots of plant conditions, seems to be a little like the common cold in humans. It won't affect production too much, especially at the end of the season, and is no reason to kill the plant!

When you finally get that first squash in the fall, it will taste sweet and the texture will be wonderful. Do be sure to buy a variety of seed that has good flavour and will store well. Your own compost seedlings from last year's dinner are probably "crosses" and won't taste as good for the space they take up, but eat them anyway!

Squashes are originally from the South American jungles, so you can imagine why they like the damp heat of the compost box. They also appreciate being in a greenhouse, if you have a big one that the pollinators can enter. I plant my squash seeds indoors and take them out when they're as tall as my hand. To hold all the goodness in, I plant them in big old sunken school bus brake drums I have filled with rotted manure and compost and soaked with diluted manure tea. Then I put a plant cap (see "Types of Greenhouses, in a Nutshell" in chapter 11) on them and go away for a couple of weeks. By then the plants are pushing against the plant cap and I lift it off, but I watch for slugs until the squashes are well on their way. I keep drenching the sunken drum with manure tea or water. If you haven't yet acquired a taste for squash, make a point of planting some anyway. Home-grown squash seems sweeter than the store-bought stuff. It's a very

## Squash love

I can always wow new gardeners by telling them, quite masterfully, why their squash plants aren't producing fruit even though they are covered with flowers. I point out that all the existing flowers are female and there are no males around yet. I wait until the exclamations die down, and then I lean over and show the suitably impressed greenhorns that behind each female flower, where it joins the stem, there is a tiny little green fruit just waiting to be pollinated. The male flower, on the other hand, joins the stem like any normal flower. Male flowers, for some reason, don't start showing up until many of the females have looked at their watches, thrown up their hands in despair and expired with lonely gasps. Sigh. But suddenly the doors blow open and the males begin showing up in a rush. Fortunately, there are a few patient females waiting about for those eager where's-the-party guys, some heavy pollinating happens, and the next thing you know there's a big, gnarly squash where that tender flower once was. Isn't love grand?

nutritious food that will keep for much of the winter, and it's cheap to grow. It'll be worth your while to find a variety you like.

### Zucchinis

Most new gardeners can coax a zucchini to produce for them, and they make a big, satisfying heap in the garden, and there are lots of recipes for using them. Since they are from the squash family, they want their seeds planted inside where it's warm, and kept warm and protected outside until true summer hits. I heard a hint once that removing up to a third of your zucchini leaves will help the plant produce more without affecting its health. The reason is that most plants produce more leaves than they need, assuming that animals will eat some of them, so they should have some extra ones for backup. But they have to supply all those leaves with water and nutrients, even if they don't need them. So go ahead, act like a grazing cow and pluck off the odd leaf from your sprawling squash plants of all types. Snap off the ones in the paths first, and then pick off leaves that are shading ripening fruit, especially as fall comes near.

## Tomatillos and plum tomatoes

You may not get a good beefsteak tomato, or even a relatively normal one, due to the "blights and wilts" that seem to kill off our vines every year. But that doesn't mean you can't bypass the struggle and move right onto some of the tomato family that *will* grow through thick and thin. The cherry tomatoes are difficult to slice for sandwiches, but will provide you with tangy fruit while the other ones fail, so look for a smaller tomato when you're reviewing the catalogues. Also look for seeds labelled "plum," "roma" or "sauce" tomatoes. These things can get the blight just like the rest of them but still pump out some usable fruit. They're good on sandwiches (even better than the "regulars," in my opinion) and in salad and hey! You can still make sauce out of what's left later! They seem to produce better in poor soil and neglect, too.

### Summer squash vs. winter squash — what gives?

What's the difference between summer and winter squash? The name doesn't actually relate to the season in which you grow them, but rather, to the season in which they are eaten! Zucchinis are generally eaten in what is truly an immature state and are at the right, tender stage in the summertime. Many other squashes develop quite a thick skin, one that is difficult to dent with the thumbnail and helps them to retain their integrity well into the winter, so that when you chop one open it is still moist and alive. Since zucchini, pattypan and crookneck squashes don't form the tremendously thick skin that Hubbard and turban squashes do, they are eaten earlier in the season and are called "summer" squashes, even when you eat them in the fall. There are no fall squashes. Don't ask.

A Mexican relative of the tomato, tomatillos can live through thick and thin. They produce well, and can be eaten raw or chopped up for salsa. So pick up a packet of these to share with a friend, and at least you'll have something to eat while your buddies are all whining about the blights and the wilts. Start your seeds indoors in mid-spring and put them out when the soil is warm — beans and squash time. They would prefer some compost in the soil but, if space gets short, tuck some tomatillos in odd corners — they're pretty tough! See also "Tomatoes" on page 43.

## SOME TRICKY VEGETABLES (FOR THE NOT QUITE SO FAINT OF HEART)

Actually, I'd be the last one to discourage anyone from planting anything they wanted, so don't let this list restrict you. Many first-year gardeners have had wild successes. But if you are struggling with fear of failure, I'd start with this batch before attempting cauliflower, celery, eggplants or melons.

### Beets

Although it is hard to get beets to come out perfectly (while you're learning how to keep your soil consistently moist, for instance), they have the redeeming quality of having great leaves to pinch off for salads. Once you get used to them as a salad food, you may end up not bothering with the roots. And if you leave them in all winter, you'll have fresh early leaves to start eating again in the spring! But if you have a nice loose, well-fed patch of soil, put in some beet seeds and keep them evenly moist all summer, using mulch and consistent watering habits. The seeds develop in a clump, so a few beets will grow quite close together no matter how carefully you sow. You can tweak out individual plants with a tiny stick and plant them farther apart, and they will grow a bit bigger than they would have. If you thin them again and eat the greens and tiny baby beets, the adjoining ones will grow bigger yet, and expand into the new space and gobble up the leftover nutrients. But don't be disappointed if your first attempts are quite small and woody.

## Broccoli, cauliflower, Brussels sprouts and cabbage

Maybe it's because these plant relatives — also known as "cole" groups — all prefer a bit more compost or manure (but not too much) and a bit less lime or wood ash (but not too little) that they have been placed on the "tricky" list. They are wonderful foods, though, and you can eat the leaves, stems and flowers of them all, so even if they fail to look like the catalogue pictures, at least you can still eat all their parts at any moment. Plant these indoors in spring and move them outside when they are manageable in size. Put them in a sunny spot in good soil, mulch and "tea" them. As soon as you notice small holes forming in the leaves, spend some time each day looking for the little green worms that are hiding along the midribs and get rid of them. The moth that lays the eggs of these creatures lays for a particular period of time each summer, so once you've squished/relocated/otherwise transmogrified the current batch, that should be it.

## Carrots

Carrots are really taken for granted as a convenient food. We all sat around at a gardening meeting one night, saying cheeky things such as "Carrots! Yes, great, must have 'em" and "Yup, nothing like a home-grown carrot," when one of us, Ron, asked if anyone had actually grown a carrot. It sounded like a silly question and we all looked at him incredulously. But he had a point. We'd grown forked, twisted, wormy and half-size carrots, but nothing like those in the stores.

So I used my best carrot-growing skills to show Ron how easy it could be. I blended compost and sand into good gardening soil and sifted it into some foot-deep wooden boxes. I planted the carrot seeds in April and kept them moist but bright. As they germinated I thinned them and weeded, still keeping the soil consistently moist. As they grew I added mulch, and kept them thinned and weeded. Finally, in midsummer I started pulling them and eating them. They were delicious, but quite small. I took one to Ron. He said, "Is this a carrot?" Okay. They were *quite* puny. Try the above methods yourself, in boxes or buckets, and see if you can get carrots past the puny stage.

## Corn

Corn takes up a lot of room and likes plenty of manure and compost, but if you have the space (corn likes to grow in a square so that the wind can blow its pollen from plant to plant) you may as well try it. One disadvantage with corn is that if the crop does fail (no big juicy ears in late summer!) you have used up quite a bit of yard, manure and water, and have no edible bits to salvage for your lost resources. Oh, well. Corn dolls, anyone?

## Spring greens (lettuces, gai lan, bok choy, corn salad, etc.)

You thought you knew about biological time clocks? Wait till you start messing with spring greens! You think you'll throw in a row or two for salads, sandwiches and stir-fries for the summer and *whamo!* The stuff flies out of the ground, looks young and luscious for a while, gets mature and beautiful for about three days, then "bolts" into seed and promptly turns bitter and nasty. Sounds like a friend of mine, actually. Anyway, you can get more mileage out of your spring greens by planting some in trays indoors, and some outside every couple of weeks, and then transplanting the indoor stuff outdoors, hoping to give yourself a longer season. You could also try planting some of the seeds in the shadier parts of the yard so that they aren't as affected by the heat. This won't work with bok choy, though.

Some plants are sensitive to hours of dark and light to tell them when to go to seed and, the minute the summer solstice hits, your bok choy will immediately begin to go to seed, like after about two days. You could set your calendar by this stuff, because it is sensitive pretty well down to seconds of light and dark. Fortunately, all the bok choy you didn't eat will send up quite edible and very pretty flowers, so do put them in your salads! If you have only one variety of Chinese green, leave a couple of plants until the seeds are dry and store those over winter.

In spring, plant the seeds of all the above in flats or directly into the garden after you've softened up the top few inches by removing twigs and rocks and breaking up clumps of soil with a shovel, then raking the bed smooth again. Shake the seeds lightly onto the soil, several inches apart, and shake some more soil gently over the row. Use your foot to lightly tamp down the soil, then go away and leave them alone. Okay, leave them alone knowing that they will probably be ravaged by hundreds of salad-munching slugs the minute they show their heads.

Plant all these greens again in late August to mid-September, to get some young leaves in the fall before the frost hits.

## Tomatoes

There are so many blights and wilts around that growing a healthy tomato plant to old age is becoming very difficult. But go ahead and plant some, and feel free to complain a lot about the results. Just don't blame the poor tomato plant, which is thousands of miles away from its real home, and didn't ask to come here in the first place. The same advice goes for eggplants and peppers. In good years, many people actually harvest some, but for the newcomer they may be a source of disappointment.

Some hints: start the seed in a warm and bright environment; give them a gentle manure-tea watering when they are young; keep them consistently warm through their youth, in a greenhouse or against a warm wall; mulch them so that

## "Ask Astilbe"

**Q:** My dad grows his tomatoes on stakes and says the process yields better fruit. Okay, it does. But why, Astilbe, why? Is my dad really that smart?

**A:** Your dad *is* smart, but I'm sure you tell him that all the time. Tying tomatoes, squashes, cucumbers and even some of your floppy flowers to wooden stakes or bamboo poles will keep the plants off the damp, cool ground where they might rot, mildew or ripen unevenly. It also keeps them out of the reach of slugs. The veggies, meanwhile, get a nice, even exposure to heat and sunlight, and who knows, they may even like the view.

rain won't splash infected soil up onto the leaves and to keep them out of the rain. Or let Bill grow them, and shower him with appreciation when he brings you a basket of them in August. See also "Tomatillos and plum tomatoes" on page 39.

### Some tomato types

> **Cherry** tomatoes are, obviously, the size of cherries, which can sometimes be smaller than you'd like — on the other hand, small tomatoes normally ripen earlier in the season, so are less of a challenge to get past the dry spells and the "blights"

> **Cluster** tomatoes are bigger than cherry tomatoes, but still ripen earlier than big ones

> **Plum** and **sauce** tomatoes are smallish, plum-size, and not as watery as the bigger types, but, more likely to squeeze out some fruit before fall. All sauce tomatoes can be used for normal eating, and all "normal" tomatoes can be used for sauce; you'll just have to cook them longer to boil off the extra water they carry in their cells

> **Beefsteak** tomatoes are those tasty, giant things that come only of a long, steady summer and early fall, and are the thing of legend. Bill grows them. He's a show-off

> Your seed package might have the word **determinate** or **indeterminate** on it. Determinate tomatoes are best for containers and small gardens, and indeterminates will keep growing like wild things, all over your paths, until winter

# AND THE NEXT STEP — HOW TO PLANT A SEED

For some reason, this important step in gardening really stops folks cold. The actual moment of opening a package and placing that frail, defence-less little object into the cold, cruel dirt to fend for itself seems to cause dismay for most of us, espe-cially the first few times out. Relax, they've been doing this longer than you have! First, let yourself recall that most of the plants growing wild around you started from seed, and without anyone to water and protect them, either. Not all wild seeds germinate, of course, and it's easy to see where our ancient forebears got the idea of placing the seeds gently onto some soft, moist ground, dusting a little dirt over top of them, and shooing away the birds and slugs until the plants could make a go of it.

You know now that the soil must be soft enough to permit air and root movement, and that it must be moist enough to support a young plant. We can help the spring bed along by pulling away all the mulch, sprouting weeds and rocks, and by turning the soil with a shovel. We can break up the clumps of soil with the shovel edge. The deeper we dig and more finely we break the clumps, the farther the roots can go without working hard, so you can make up your mind about how much help you feel like giving them. And since you're standing there with a shovel, you may as well scatter compost, crushed seashells and aged manure over the plot and dig that in as you go.

### When to plant

The following table will tell you when to plant your seeds:

| When | Where | What |
| --- | --- | --- |
| March | Indoors in seed trays | Tomatoes, cabbage, broccoli, herbs |
| March | Outside | Peas, carrots, potatoes, lettuce, radishes, bok choy, gai lan, onions, spinach, beets |
| April | Indoors | Squash, peppers |
| Early May | Outside | Beans, tomatoes, squash, corn, cucumber |
| Fall | Outside | Leeks, garlic, potatoes, lettuce, green onion sets, radishes |

## There are several ways to actually plant a seed

Much is said about the appropriate planting depth of seeds, so let's handle that here. The dispute seems to hinge on whether to plant the seed at a depth of two or three times its diameter. I've seen people discuss this heatedly, plant the seed at twice its diameter, then water gently and watch the seed become exposed (i.e., at no times its diameter).

The seed doesn't know if it is two, three or even four times its diameter under the ground. All it knows is how darn long it seems to be taking to get to the surface. That's about all there is to it. If it gets planted too deeply, it will just take a longer time to get to ground level. This is actually used as a winter growing technique for peas. Plant them a full six inches deep in the fall and by spring they'll appear, a little tuckered out but ready to roll.

On the other hand, if a seed is not planted deeply enough the sprout may topple over. In that case, put your finger tips onto the surface of the soil around the plant, push down firmly but gently, then push a little more soil around the exposed stem to hold it up. Experimentation will teach you a lot about the "touch" this will require.

### Three simple planting methods

➧ After levelling out the soil with a rake, use the handle lengthwise to make a small depression, drop the seeds in, and use your fingers to cover them with soil. Water gently

➧ Place the seed on the loosened soil. Step on it. Go away

➧ The indoor way to plant a seed is to fill a small tray that has holes in it with sifted, moist soil, and press the seed into the soil. Place the tray in a clear bag, blow air into it and twist-tie it. Place it in a warm spot with good reflected light (so you don't cook the little blighters). When the plants sprout, take them out of the bag and give them gentle watering until they're big enough to put outside

The seed packet will tell you if the seeds need light to germinate, in which case you just scatter them onto the soil, press them gently and keep them moist. Some people worry about planting flat seeds, such as pumpkin, and about which side is up. Don't worry, seedlings are like beetles and will flip themselves over in the soil. This is another reason to keep your soil loose by mulching, and not treading on it.

Most seeds benefit from an overnight soaking to start them on their passage, so give that a try. Just put them in a bowl with some warm water, and don't forget to leave the seed package under the bowl so you'll know which type you're soaking. This is only convenient for the larger seeds, because the tiny ones are too hard to plant when they're wet. Yes, some seeds do need to think they've had winter before they will germinate, and so need a spell in the fridge, but most of our annual garden vegetables started off in warmer climates and don't need any special treatment to wake up for spring. Remember: mark your planting area to show where and what you've seeded.

## PLANTING PROBLEMS

### Keep it moist

The most common problem for gardeners is not the act of putting the seeds in the soil but keeping that top half inch of soil damp until the seed

## "Ask Astilbe"

**Q:** I use sterilized soil for my seedlings, but I still get damping-off disease (causing all my seedlings to fall over) every spring. How can I avoid this without fungicides?

**A:** Amazingly enough, if you stop using sterilized soil, you can avoid fungal diseases. But how? My guess is that soil, being a living thing, contains its own anti-fungal properties. When we sterilize the soil we kill the "anti-fungalness." Then we expose the soil to all the passing drafts containing – you guessed it – spores that can now grow on the lovely moist medium with impunity. Of course, your "seed mix" salesperson will not want to discuss this. One advantage of buying sterilized soil is that it doesn't contain viable weed seeds, so you won't end up growing a batch of plants you just spent the previous summer pulling out. But you can sterilize your own soil. Choose a site where the plants grew well, and shovel up some scoops of the dirt there. Sift the soil to remove the rocks and sticks (and return the worms to the garden). Heat the sifted soil in a roasting pan in the oven for one hour at 200°F (I really know how to thrill a guy with my cooking). When the soil is cool, fill, plant and water your flats. Then pop them right into plastic bags, blow air into them and set them in a bright, warm spot. My own method is to use nonsterilized, sifted garden soil, and pick out the recognizable weeds as they appear. This is the only negative aspect I have discovered to using raw soil. Damping-off disease? I've seen so little of it, that it isn't an issue, and when I do see some I move my plants to a brighter, better-ventilated area.

has sprouted roots, so that it can dive for its own water. Mulch the planting area with a shallow layer of hay or dried grass, or place some damp newspaper or cardboard over the planting area, and keep that damp. Pull it up gently to check for growth, and remove it when things are on the way. After the seedlings are up, water well and start putting a layer of hay, leaves or dried grass around the area, leaving a space around the stem to check for slugs. Once you see the young plant surge forward, you can relax a bit.

## A true planting story

After buying myself a very scientific book on how to germinate confusing seeds, I finally received some wonderful and exotic barberry seeds from England. I hesitated to plant them because I couldn't find the specific variety in my new book and didn't know whether they had to think it was winter (and thus be put in the fridge), or spring, winter, and then spring again, as some seeds do. If they did need to have spring, winter and spring, how long should each false season be? And maybe I should heat them first, maybe I should soak them and then heat them. Or maybe they needed to be swirled in warm, dilute acid under a full moon and then spat on by a raven. It didn't matter, really, because I lost the packet. I found it weeks later in the greenhouse when I lifted a big clay pot and discovered the crumpled, sodden seed packet. I ripped it open and every single seed had germinated. I planted them, and they all grew.

## Is that for me?

The second biggest problem with planting is keeping the bugs, slugs and birds away until the new plant can survive a bit of damage. Chapter 9 on pests will provide some detailed help with this problem.

## The gift of light

If you're starting seeds indoors, providing adequate light is a problem. If you don't have grow lights, put your trays right under a desk lamp with a grow bulb, or under a strip of fluorescent bulbs, or right inside a newspaper-shielded window. Place them outdoors in a protected spot on sunny days. Start new seeds right away if you have failures.

## And finally –

Remember that the seed has only one plan, and that is to grow. If it has the four essentials and a bit of time, it will be fine. Pay some attention to these needs in the first part of your plant's life and it will grow vigorously later on. Trust in the seed. It wants to grow.

# THE HERB GARDEN

## 5

Growing herbs is so straightforward that when it was suggested that I include a chapter on them, I stretched my brain (not a pretty picture) to think of something that (1) wasn't just another tedious fact already in all the other gardening books and (2) was useful and exciting for the beginner.

The two things that hit me right away were that it doesn't matter how much you know about herbs, if you don't integrate them into your life properly it doesn't matter if you have them or not, and that I must impress upon you that herbs ("herb" just means a plant used for medicine or flavouring) come from different parts of the world and each needs the right planting spot so that it can serve you happily.

## HOW TO GET MORE OUT OF YOUR HERB GARDEN

Herb gardens are a lot like hot tubs. People want them, but once they're installed they don't get used much. Okay, maybe herb gardens aren't a *lot* like hot tubs, but the point stands. We get taken to a friend's new garden and are formally shown the herb bed. Everyone nods happily and heads back to the house, making kind comments. The problem? Everyone's hands should be full! Herbs are for living in, smelling and eating and strewing (should that come up).

### Getting more excited about herbs (without actually having a fit)

You don't have to know how to make essential oils to really get a charge out of your herbs. Just rubbing your hands through a heady batch of tarragon, rosemary and lemon verbena should raise you to a state in which it's dangerous to operate heavy machinery. Beyond their stupefying effects they have lots of practical uses, though, so here is a list of my personal favourites and easy ways to use them.

### Basil

Beginners get disappointed with basil because it needs a different touch than the other herbs. It's a warm-weather annual, and you should start it indoors and then keep it protected, whether in a greenhouse or a sunny, sheltered spot where it can soak up the heat all day. Although it will appreciate a quick-draining spot like a sandy patch, it still wants to be watered regularly. Once it takes off, start eating. Pinch the tips off it and eat those first, and that will help keep the plant bushy. Cut off whole branches for particular dishes as the plant grows.

---

**Pesto Sauce — that yummy, freeze-able way to keep basil around all winter**

1/2 cup packed clean basil leaves
2 cloves garlic (or more, if you're a freak for it)
1/4 cup crushed walnuts or pine nuts
1/2 cup olive oil
A blender and an ice cube tray

Blend the leaves, garlic and nuts into a chopped mess, then add the olive oil until the mix becomes smooth. Add salt to taste. This is meant to be a thick mixture, not really a sauce. Pour into ice cube trays and freeze. Dump the cubes into bags for freezer storage. Heat and serve with Parmesan cheese over pasta, with bread and a salad.

## Borage

Sprawling, pretty with its bright blue flowers, great for attracting bees to the garden. I'm going to plant borage in my strawberry bed this year because it's supposed to have a great mutually beneficial effect. All above-ground parts are edible, but I haven't been tempted to eat the leaves raw or cooked, as suggested, because of the prickles, because I'm a sissy, and because I have lots of other options. But I sure do use the flowers in salads and as garnish on devilled eggs. These plants grow easily from seed, but don't like being moved once they get going.

## Camomile

Pretty little plant where you need a short sun-lover. Famous as a calming tea, and the bags can then be used on the eyes to perk them up, or as a compress on wounds. Also good for perking up plants around it wherever it is planted.

## Chives

If you aren't using your chives all the time, dig up your patch and move it as close to your kitchen entrance as possible. Or plant some in a big pot and keep it on the porch. Get in the habit of cutting chives into the morning scrambled eggs and the evening salad and potatoes. Toss them finely cut onto your melted-cheese sandwich or steamed veggies and stir-fries. You'll get addicted to that small nip of flavour. Chives can be eaten at any stage and the flowers are tasty, too. The flowers' stalks are tough and can be left with the plant. Chives are totally low-maintenance and come back every year, without your help.

## Dill

Yum — pinch the leaves off for potato salad or steamed potatoes, herb butters, herb breads, fish dishes, salads. Of course, the flower heads are famous for flavouring pickled cukes and beans. Dill is a funny plant in that it grows only where it wants to, and then grows like crazy forever more. If your dill patch has failed in the past, find some tiny babies in a friend's yard and transplant them carefully to where you want them. Don't pick all the seed heads off the first year, because you want them to re-establish for you next year.

## Greek oregano

I love this stuff. I cut my plants back when they get more than six inches tall and take the cuttings inside to dry. This way I prepare enough through the summer to carry me through the winter, and the plants don't seem to mind. I keep a jar in the kitchen and put ample amounts into every pasta dish I cook, as well as over salads, pizza-style dishes and anything else with cheese and tomatoes. Oregano seems to prefer a well-drained warm spot, and I mulch it in the winter for some added protection. Of all the marjoram family, the Greek oregano has the strongest flavour.

# Lavender

Used in everything from ice cream to bathwater or just as a dried bouquet in the bathroom, lavender may simply just sit there and look pretty. The bushes get old and die, so be ready with a new baby when yours starts looking peaked. The proper time to cut the flowers of this famous herb is just before you think you should, when they are still snug to the stem. If you pick them when they're fully open they will fall apart when they're really dry. It's best to plant lavender in a hot, dry, well-drained area.

# Lemon balm

Another good tea and salad plant, and I use lots of it in flower arrangements. The easily eaten leaf can be incorporated into summer drinks and desserts. Basically, this is another easy plant that doesn't need a lot of fuss. It will self-seed all over the yard.

# Mints

If you want a taste experience, cut the top five or six inches off a peppermint plant so that you have a ball of herb that will fit into your fist. Drop it into a teapot and fill the pot with boiling water. You will be amazed at the power of the oils in this tea, and may become a convert. Use these very edible leaves in desserts and salads, and snip them over new potatoes. Garnish food trays and flavour cold drinks. Throw leaves into your bathwater, or just tuck sprigs into your buttonhole when you're gardening. The mints are a big family, but the most popular types are peppermint and spearmint. Both are tough, and you may want to plant them in pots recessed into the ground so that they don't completely run away on you. I've got mine in a wild part of the garden, though, where they are allowed to go free.

**The mint collector**

If you have a damp, shady spot in your yard, consider starting a mint collection. Begin with the big, robust, reddish peppermint, add the more delicate spearmint, and then find a sample of the variegated apple mint, which is a nice plant just for show and is great in cut flowers. There are ginger mints and curly leaved ones, orange-scented ones, lemon-scented ones, and the famous *Eau de cologne*. There is even a chocolate-scented variety. Collect all 600 varieties (no kidding!).

## Parsley

This is the classic garden herb that is chopped onto potatoes and eggs or tucked behind orange slices and around fish dishes. It is known for its ability to freshen the breath and its antiseptic properties as a poultice for infected wounds (don't think of this when it's on your plate). Parsley is a biennial, so you will have to plant it two years in a row, and wait for it to seed in alternate years, to keep a constant supply growing in your yard.

## Rosemary

I could sit there by the bush with my nose stuck into it, but I wouldn't get anything done. And I admit my actual use of it is wildly reduced now that I rarely consume little lambies. But it is still good in herb butters for veggie dishes, and in potatoes and salads, and can be used in a facial steam, or just brought in to perfume the air. You can merely stuff your face into it on the way by, if you have the time. Rosemary likes a sunny wall to lean against, and might like mulching in winter if you expect lots of freezing. Make sure your soil drains well, wherever you put this herb.

## Tarragon

Eggs, herb butters, fish dishes, salad dressings and flavoured vinegars. Tarragon can "go bad" and completely lose its scent, but when it's working, it certainly is something you could inhale deeply for some time. Look for French tarragon when buying plants, but don't turn down the tougher Russian plants if that is what you can find. Tarragon doesn't dry well, but can be frozen in ice cube trays.

## Thyme

This is another herb that is nice in pasta dishes, with or without the tomatoes. Just cut a few inches off the end of a branch and pluck the little leaves into your cooking pot with your fingernails. Thyme is great because it's usable all winter long, so you don't have to worry so much about drying a supply of it. It is short enough to plant along the front of a sunny bed.

## MORE USES

Just about every herb can be used as a tea, and they generally also have quite wonderful medicinal uses. But I won't go into medicinals in this book because it is such a huge and important subject, and the idea of a *Medicinal Plants for the Faint of Heart* has an ominous ring to it, somewhat like *Brain Surgery for the Faint of Heart*.

If you're curious, you could start with something like *The Complete Book of Herbs* by Lesley Bremness, and work your way into more complexity when you are ready. Herbs are also capable of creating dyes — another great big topic. And they attract beneficial insects to the garden, and you don't have to memorize anything to enjoy that!

## Drying herbs

Herb-drying can be stretched into a very exact science, but here is the tolerable, usable lowdown. If you pick herbs when they are wet and hang them in the dark, they can mildew. That's why it is recommended that all herbs be picked for drying when there is no water on them at all.

**Keep these jars or bags out of bright light and heat**
Although the books go on and on about ideal humidity and brightness for drying, I find there's a wide range of very tolerable situations, so don't let a questionable environment stop you from drying some herbs. Just do it, and let your success pull you toward perfection later on.

**Herb baths**

Any herb whose smell you enjoy can be added to your bathwater. Cleaning the tub can take longer if you just throw the leaves in, so you have a choice of making a pot of tea with the herbs and just straining the teapot into the bathwater, or tying the herbs in a piece of fabric and hanging it under the tap.

➧ Sleepy-time bath: hops, jasmine, valerian

➧ Wake-up bath: mints, basil, lemon balm, rosemary, sage, thyme

There are a lot of other plants and combinations, but the key element should be that you enjoy the scent. For that reason you should avoid chives, for instance, or the decidedly unromantic "pizza bath" — oregano, anyone?

If you are actually stuck and must, for instance, leave for Spuzzum at first light, pick the herbs but give them a good shake, roll them loosely in a dishtowel to get off more water, and hang them in very loose bunches for the day. Otherwise, wait for the sun to dry the dew off them, like a good traditionalist.

There is also an exact science of deciding at which part of the season to pick each herb, based on when its oils are at their highest level. This would be important if you were making medicinals, but I hate to see the average home grower leave oregano or mint out of the recipe because it's the wrong time of year to gather it! Pick the stuff! Use it now! You'll learn yourself by picking when each of the herbs smells best. The rule of thumb is that the oils are at their peak just before flowering, but some medicinals are prepared after flowering, which throws that rule of thumb out the window (ouch). As I say, rub and sniff the leaves. If they smell good, pick and dry them. Check each piece carefully so that you can discard buggy leaves before they show up in the teapot. I don't have a drying rack, so I tie bunches, however small, with elastic bands that will contract along with the stem. I hang these clumps over any available protuberance in my darkish but well-ventilated guestroom. When I run out of protuberances, I just lay newspaper on the desk and begin drying leaves and seeds there. An airy shed or carport (minus the exhaust fumes) would do. I keep a stack of small pieces of paper and a pen handy, so that I can mark each clump as it comes in. If I don't have this paper ready, I will never tag the plants and will have to do the "sniff" test later, which is not always dependable. When the clumps are dry enough to crumble in my fingers (and before the spiderwebs and dust layers begin to set), I strip the leaves into a brown bag or jar, but I don't mash them up small because I want the oils to stay as intact as possible inside the leaf. Don't crush the leaves until you actually add them to your recipe!

**Herb butters**

Finely chop your chives, parsley, oregano, thyme or whatever you desire, and blend four tablespoons of the fresh herb with each quarter cup of butter.

# Herb oils

If you want the distinctive scent of the herb to shine through, use an unscented oil like safflower, but if the herb will be used in recipes with olive oil (such as the Mediterranean herbs — oregano, lavender, rosemary, thyme — that are part of the cooking that originated with olive oil), use the olive oil as your base. Or mix the oils, if you can't make up your mind! Pick your herbs when the dew has dried and check them for bugs or dirt. Make sure your container is extremely clean and loosely fill one-third of it with your herbs or herb combinations. Top up the container with the oil, cover it and let it sit in a dark place for two weeks. If it doesn't smell strongly by the end of two weeks, strain the oil, add fresh herbs and try another week. When you're satisfied, strain out the herbs with cheesecloth or a good

| Plant | Sunny | Some shade | Sandy soil | Healthy soil |
|---|---|---|---|---|
| Basil | √ | | | √ |
| Borage | √ | | √ | |
| Camomile | √ | | √ | |
| Chervil | √ | √ | √ | |
| Chives | √ | √ | | √ |
| Coriander/cilantro | √ | | | √ |
| Cicely | | √ | | √ |
| Dill | √ | | | √ |
| Fennel | √ | | | √ |
| Hyssop | √ | | √ | |
| Lemon balm | √ | √ | √ | √ |
| Lemon verbena | √ | | √ | √ |
| Lavender | √ | | √ | |
| Mint and catnip | | √ | | √ |
| Oregano | √ | | √ | |
| Parsley | √ | √ | | √ |
| Rosemary | √ | | √ | |
| Rue | √ | √ | √ | |
| Sage | √ | | √ | |
| Savory | √ | | | √ |
| Tarragon | √ | | | √ |
| Thyme | √ | | √ | |

strainer and tightly bottle the oil. Keep the oil cool and in a dark place. Although all my pictures of herb oil show the pretty herbs still in the bottle, all my recipes suggest taking them out so they don't turn a nasty shade of brown.

## Right place, right thyme

There is a broad assumption that herbs should be planted in a sunny, well-drained bed. If the plant developed over centuries on a rocky hillside in southern Europe, it will like a sunny, well-drained bed. But if it naturalized along the mucky riverbanks of northern Europe, as did mint, it will need damper, cooler, richer soil.

Therefore, you will need *at least* two herb gardens because, like people we know, different types thrive best in different locations. There should be one nicely drained, sunny spot for the Mediterranean herbs and a moister, cooler place near the tree edges or fences for the plants that developed in forest glades.

There are plenty that could live happily in the middle, so your midrange spot could be ideal for a third bed. Herbs can also be planted throughout the garden wherever the right site offers itself, because they are famous "companion" plants that can scare away bugs with their smells or pull up interesting nutrients for the other plants to share.

Like all plants, herbs should be moved or planted in the spring or fall when the earth is moist, so that their roots can get established without stress. Go ahead and plant in midsummer if you can keep that plant, even the Mediterranean ones, nice and moist and mulched for a couple of months to help it to "take."

# A FEW OF MY FAVOURITE FLOWERS

## 6

## THEY'RE BEAUTIFUL, THEY'RE TOUGH, AND THEY DON'T NEED ME – I LOVE THEM

My appreciation for flowers was a slow affair, with a sudden stumbling upon some amazing bit of beauty here and there, with my growing appreciation for colour and texture in art, and the awe-inspiring realization that plants were completely portable. Something I truly loved could be gently dug up (and not always in the dark of night) and relocated to where I could appreciate it all the time. It was that final point that turned me into a plant junkie. I wanted a bit of that burnt orange right here! And some of those tiny bits of red mixed in over there. It made me even more aware of what each new plant would offer by way of a flowering part. But the practical cat in me is always in conflict with the gooey flower babe, so I am now trying to figure out which of my favourite flowers are also edible, medicinal, or good for companion planting. Don't worry about me, though, I can think of an excuse to ease in another showy flower if I need to.

Which would I choose if I really had to suggest them to a new gardening friend? Darn, now I'm going to have to sit on the couch, surrounded by plant books for two or three nights, looking at all the pretty pictures and mulling over possibilities. I hate it when that happens. But a woman's got to do what a woman's got to do, so please join me on a brief journey through a fantasy garden, with a few modest (and easy to find) country cousins thrown in.

By the way, although all gardening paths do finally end up leading to tricky Latin terms, we are going to avoid them here for as long as possible. Your first challenge is going to be to identify and enjoy the plants that are already around you, and then one by one, you can add their Latin monikers to your expanding botanical vocabulary. After all, do you really want me to tell you not to plant your *Hemerocallis fulva* so close to your *Eschsholzia caepitosa* (and that hue next to the *Tagetes tenuifolia* — really darling!)? I didn't think so! And I certainly wouldn't get invited to the really fun dinner parties, talking like that.

## Asiatic lilies

Huge soft trumpets that exude an incredible scent, on plants that you stick in the ground, swat the slugs off in spring and basically walk away from. Mulch so that the soil doesn't get dry, and give them a drop of "poo tea" — that's all you have to know. They come in many scents and softly melting hues. Buy yourself some bulbs today!

## Centaurea montana

Sorry, just had to slip a Latin name in there. You might find them called Mountain Cornflower. These make two-foot clumps of blue-and-pink flowers, which are wonderful with other pink flowers in an arrangement. Nothing seems to bother them, and they will run amok in your garden and come up everywhere. Give them away as gifts.

## Day lilies

So named because each flower lasts for only one day, these flowers grow from a central clump and not on a single long stalk like the Asiatic lilies. Day lilies are, like many of my favourite things, not codependent, and will do their own thing for years. And you can eat 'em, which you can't do with the usual codependents. Eat young roots, shoots or flowers raw, cook old roots and shoots. Mulch around them to keep the weeds back, and rip them apart from year to year to share or move around the yard.

### Annuals vs. perennials — what gives?

These terms are used a lot in garden conversation so you may as well get comfortable with them. Here's the lowdown: an annual is a plant that grows from seed in the springtime, grows a root and stem, and when those are both the right size, produces a flower head. The flower head then goes through the usual process of pollinating, dying, then leaving behind a brown, wizened seed head. By winter, it's all over but the blues. The stem and root die and dissolve. The bitter winds blow the seed head down into the cold, wet earth, where it lies shivering until spring warmth prompts it to sprout. Then the whole process begins again. Perennials do things differently. They can begin from a seed or a cutting, and then grow a root and stem just like the annual. Things usually stop there for the winter. In spring, the plant grows some more, and may finally put out a flower, which does all the usual stuff with bees, then the flower dies, the seeds fall to the ground … but the roots live on! And each year, the roots produce a bigger system — more stems, more flowers. Some perennials take a few years to mature enough to create a flower. There! That's the starter edition. Now go out and identify some plants!

## Hollyhocks

The ones in my garden grow about six feet tall and have crinkled burnt-peach-coloured flowers for a few weeks, wonderful texture, and are striking and majestic — oh, stop me, *please!* Okay, I'm nauseating myself, but I always drag my friends around to the back when the hollyhocks are in bloom. Don't worry if they get "rust"; just break off the worst parts and let them go on. They'll come back next year all right.

## Italian arums

These are really hard to find, unless you live near me and travel at night with a flashlight. I love arums because they can pop up in fall, winter or spring with big, tropical-looking leaves totally encased in ice, or live in wet shade on the north side of the house, so that at the oddest times of the year these wonderful things are gracing the front door. In summer the leaves die down, making way for all the other shade plants in the bed, and they put up a stick covered in orange berries that last quite a long time.

## Roses

Have a red rose bush and a yellow rose bush. Buy a blue glass vase (turquoise — trust me). Whenever possible, put a red and a yellow rose in the vase. Put it on a windowsill. Sit and look at it and drink tea. This will raise you to a new level. Trust me. Meanwhile, mulch and feed your roses and cut back any sappy, spindly growth in early spring until you find out what kinds of roses you have. Since roses bloom on new growth, cutting the old stuff back won't hurt them.

## Teasel

I admit these are hard to find as young plants, and you only need a couple so a whole seed packet is a waste (give them to Bill), but WHOOWEE! These are not pretty plants, but they are show-stoppers that really make you think about what

**When do vegetables have flowers?**

Always! Flowers and vegetables are presented separately in seed catalogues and in books, but don't forget that all vegetables have flowers, even parsnips and onions, peas and broccoli, and it is only a matter of size and flair that keeps these blooms from getting noticed. If you want to add a twist to your next picnic table bouquet, throw in some dramatic parsnip or fennel umbels, or a huge sprig of rhubarb flower, or use the kale and broccoli flowers for a bright yellow spray. Look closely at your pea and potato flowers — it's a new, tiny and subtle world down there.

maketh the flower and about the whole wonder of plant diversity. Plant one in a far corner where the spines won't bother you, and then watch the show the second year as the totally freaky, artsy flowers appear and turn into permanent reminders of the Stone Age. Or another planet. They grow about seven feet tall and need no special care as far as I can see.

## Crocosmia

After hacking at some overgrown brush one spring on my old property, some green spikes began to arise at that spot. As summer wore on and they grew, they began to produce long stems bearing red flowers. This went on for years, with no help from me, so I brought them with me to my new property and now I'm even nice to them and mulch them once in a while. They are dramatic as a cut flower because they last a long time.

## "Ask Astilbe"

**Q:** Okay, Astilbe, my aunt has a "cutting" garden full of flowers, but I have a flower garden, too, and she won't call it a "cutting" garden even though I cut flowers all the time. Is my aunt a plant snob? Is it genetically encoded? Should I worry?

**A:** Nope, but you should rush right over there with your transplanting equipment and see what she's got! She probably chose which plants she wanted by how well the flowers held up after they were cut, how stiff the stems were so that they wouldn't wilt, and how long the stems were. That's before she started worrying about the colour and size of the blooms. I bet she has delphiniums, hollyhocks and gladioli, roses and daisies and crocosmia, and Peruvian lilies, cornflowers and peonies, chrysanthemums and dahlias and carnations. And she probably uses yarrow and ferns, baby's breath, salal, sedum and lady's mantle for fillers. So while you're out there with your California poppies wilting and your violets sliding out of their vase, your aunt is enjoying the results of having chosen well for long lasting effect. Now that's role modelling! But you can always learn for yourself by taking cuttings of young, just-opening flowers from your garden, putting them quickly into cool water and taking your own notes on what held up and what didn't like it at all. You might learn something to tell her!

## Daisies

Yup, good old-fashioned daisies. I cut the biggest ones with some stems of variegated grass and put them in a white vase. I put this vase in any gloomy corner of the house and it really lights up the place. Daisies get messy by the end of the year and have to be tied up and deadheaded (blech — more scary garden terms) to keep from getting mangy, but I forgive them for the bit of light they give me all summer.

# BEDDING PLANTS

## Why is it a bedding plant, and not just a plant?

Darned if I know! The term "bedding plant" covers all those bits of colour you can pick up at the nursery in spring and settle into your flower beds (Oh! Now I get it!) for added visual pizzazz. Bedding plants are normally annuals, which we know will flower in their first year, so we can depend on them to blossom away quite dependably and for a longer period than our more programmed perennials if we remember to pinch off the faded flowers before they can form seed. They are usually short in stature, so are placed where they are easily seen along paths, in front of taller perennials, or in hanging pots or deck planters. They come in lots of colours, grow upright and hang nicely over planter edges, and have a wide variety of foliage types. You can have a lot of fun with a medium like this — arranging words, rainbows and colour scales through beds and up your staircase, or picking plants all in one hue as an accent to your windowsills or to complement your house colour.

## Cool! But ... why not?

After a long winter we are all thrilled to tuck in our bedding plants to let the spring begin, but in our urgency they frequently hit the soil before winter is truly past. Many of us end up planting

### Decorating your flowers

Flowers and foliage go together so, when you pick flowers, walk around and hold them next to different plants and see what brings out their texture and shape. I have a large clump of what I think is picta grass, a bright, variegated green-and-white grass that looks great with just about anything and lives for a long time in water. I also use strawberry leaves, bamboo branches, ferns and ivy, lemon balm and apple mint, or sage twigs to set off certain plants. Let yourself roam! In winter I use salal, those artsy, twisty huckleberry branches, and more ferns to keep my store-bought flowers company.

them twice, the second time after we've recovered from our giddiness. One thing you can do is remember that *warm* spring days, the ones where we want to plant the whole front yard, coincide with *cold*, *clear* spring nights, and possible frosts. The nursery owners must shake their heads that we fall for this every year. It is, in fact, better to plant out your little annuals at the beginning of a rainy spell, when the day/night temperatures won't swing as much and they will get adequate time to settle into damp soil before the sun comes out to cook them. But this cure introduces problem number two — bedding plants get set into the ground just as the slugs are waking up with empty tummies. All that lush young growth, so close to eager mouth parts, will offer an irresistible snack, and you will have to be hypervigilant with whatever technique you use (besides avoiding anything that will poison another creature) to keep your annuals alive during this spell. You'll soon notice that the smarter perennials will have their buds up high by the time they flower, so they are more successful at remaining intact, although their leaves may get tattered by insects.

## Geraniums

Or pelargoniums (true geraniums are hardy, but the plants we have to protect in winter are pelargoniums, but everyone calls them geraniums. Try to roll with this). These are mid-size, upright plants, and will grow a lot, so you'll have to remember to give them a good fist-size space in a container. They run through the pink, salmon and red range, and carry their flowers quite high on spikes, so they can be placed at the back of a planter. They have enough stage presence to be used alone in unique pots along a deck or railing.

## Lobelia

A small, low-growing or hanging plant that puts out many tiny blue, white or pink flowers for quite a long time into the fall. They can be very showy draped down the front of the house and do well in shade. They don't seem to need deadheading, which is great, because it would be a tedious job! Put them in the front of your container so that they drape forward and out of the way, showing off the plants behind them.

## Marigolds

These come in oranges and yellows, so they can add good spots of brightness to your planters and beds, but they need very prompt deadheading and are a favourite of slugs. They come in various heights and flower sizes, but are generally quite upright and so aren't used much in hanging baskets.

### How to choose your bedding plant

Our natural tendency as we hover over the nursery racks is to pick out the biggest plants of the batch, the ones that already have a few flowers on them and are bursting out of their pots. But good nursery folks will steer you away from these and encourage you — get this — to take home the smaller, flowerless specimen beside it. And if they can't talk you into that, they will urge you to nip the buds from your new babies! Really, what is the hope of having the brightest spring garden with advice like that? But they have a point. The bigger plants are already quite root-bound and may have exhausted the soil supply in their pots. They shouldn't be putting their energy into flowers just yet, when you really want to settle them into a new planter and encourage a quick burst of rooting by providing healthy soil and adequate water. The more chance the plant has to do this, the better show you will have. I can certainly attest to my own greed, when I tweak out a dead plant that never really made the grade, only to find that its root clump still holds the shape of a long-gone plastic pot. That's bad planting, and I always feel a pang of remorse. Then I toss the evidence into the compost and do it again next year. Sigh.

## Nasturtiums

The reason people like these so much is that they give a lot without tons of fuss. Where a whiny little petunia will sit and pout for half the summer unless you actually look after the damn thing, a nasturtium that gets its legs under it will spread and flower till frost. Go smile at them, it's all you have to do. Don't worry if yours get aphids — if that keeps them away from the broccoli, be happy. Nasturtium flowers and leaves are edible, so tear some into the salad. Like sweet peas, nasturtiums have to be planted each spring, but that's easy. Saving their strange, wrinkly seeds is no trouble.

## Pansies

I thought pansies were "old lady plants" (Mom will give me heck for that) until I spent some time looking at the flowers closely. They have a satiny, velvety texture and little cat faces and are quite pleasant to stroke while you're sitting on the steps, waiting for a ride. They come in lots of colours, seem to flower through early and late frost, and live quite well in shade. Now I line up with the other, er, mature women and pick up a four-pack in late fall to give the deck a bit more life until winter truly hits.

## Petunias

Those are the brightly coloured trumpet-shaped flowers on the little sprawling plants. They come in lots of bright colours and seem pretty happy with a tiny root space, so they're good for use in hanging pots and planters. If you keep them deadheaded, give them a bit of food and don't bake them to toast in really hot sun or let them get smashed to shreds by the rain or eaten by bugs, you will get several months of vivid and decent-size flowers.

## Sweet peas

Not big and showy, sweet peas' claim to fame is that you have to pick off the flowers as they open because that keeps the plant from going to seed. Never mind the details — what you have is a reason that you *must* pick a handful of these every few days and put them in the house so that every time you pass them their happy aroma will fill you with bliss. Plant sweet pea seeds in mid-spring and give them some net to climb — coincidentally, about up to your nose is a good height.

**Hydrate that sprout!**

Even if you pick the little ones, chances are that your nursery plants have filled their pots with roots and left very little room for moist medium (nurseries don't use soil). When you bring home your flats of young bedding plants, sit them in a pan of water for a couple of hours so that you'll be putting them into the soil full of nice, plump cells!

## Zinnias

A bit like giant marigolds, these plants grow in stiff, upright tufts and come in a wide range of colours. I find zinnias seem much more eager to live than marigolds and flower for a lot longer. Like marigolds, they're too tall and stiff to put in hanging baskets unless you get the miniatures, but are nice and strong in pots by themselves or positioned with sprawling plants draping down in front of them. It's really easy to learn about seed-saving with zinnias — just pull off a dry flower, let it dry even more, then pull it apart to gather the large, obvious seeds that are growing along the dead petals. You can plant the seeds next spring.

# A LITTLE VINE, DARLINK?

You know what to do with a blank wall, right? Use it! That's what all those silly outdoor walls, garage sides and fences are really for — to keep plants off the ground. Some plants are genetically modified to prefer this position (lateral, that is) and have tendrils or suckers, while others just twine in circles around anything upright. This obviously must benefit them as plants, but happily for us it's also good for humans! It means we can cram more botanical wonders into a small space, because a 20-foot plant can take up as little as one square foot of growing area. Naturally, all climbing plants can be dug up and moved.

## Clematis

There are lots of varieties of clematis. Some have very big, blue, showy flowers, some have smaller white ones. There's a nice evergreen variety, too, that looks great in spring. The only general rule I've heard for tending clematis is "cool feet, hot head." The idea is to keep the root area cool, by planting it around a shady corner and training the top growth into the sun, or mulching the root area and growing a low shrub around the base to keep the soil surface shaded and cool.

### Stakes and poles and netting and string

The above items are just some of the materials you can use to start a lateral or vine garden. Think about how you can attach your framework to withstand the weight and strength of a happy, growing plant. Even peas can collapse a frail old fence, once they get laden with full pods. You will need heavy twine or wire to bind the tops of poles together, stakes driven well into the ground (more than a foot deep for even a self-respecting sweet pea) and cup hooks or solidly hammered nails to hold up string and netting. The main problem with lateral growing is making the support strong enough. This is one of those occasions when going severely overboard should just about do it.

## Honeysuckle

Yes! Buy a scented honeysuckle, get a deck chair, and sit out in the late afternoon and just inhale for half an hour before dinner. Mind-expanding but not fattening, like good cheesecake. There are several varieties, almost evergreen, some highly scented, some with wild-looking orange flowers. Strip off dead or sickly branches in early spring, and then just leave your honeysuckle to go! It's easy to take a cutting by bending the stem down and pinning it to the ground.

## Hops

Yup, the type with which they make beer. All the hops types look quite alike, lose their leaves, and have strange but intriguing little papery pinecones hanging gracefully off them through the fall. Although hops "take" very quickly and grow a mass of pretty foliage all summer, they will drop their leaves in fall, leaving your ugly old fence right where you left it. Don't forget that the young shoots are edible when steamed, and that you can make beer and a sleeping mixture from the hops themselves, so they may be worth it.

### Flowers aren't just for us!

It's easy, when you're swooning in front of a beautiful plant, to forget that good looks actually have a business-like purpose — colours and shapes attract different creatures that might appreciate the food a plant offers and usually return the favour by doing some quick pollinating while they're hovering around.

**Plants that attract hummingbirds:**

Red elderberry; currant; salmonberry; beauty bush; fuchsia; clematis; honeysuckle; morning glory and trumpet vines; scarlet runner bean; petunia; zinnia and dahlia; red-hot poker; bleeding heart; columbine; delphinium and foxglove; bee balm; phlox; and cardinal flowers.

**Plants that attract butterflies:**

Oregon grape; salal; thimbleberry; red elderberry and red huckleberry; yarrow; columbine; butterfly bush; fennel and lavender; lemon balm; peppermint and spearmint; parsley and sage; and thyme and coneflower.

## Ivy

This is a famous no-care plant that can take a lot of shade and is really hardy. It can get very heavy and the plant develops persistent rootlets along its branches, so watch out when you're planting it over a rickety old carport. It's great for an evergreen

### Bulbs – the perfect gift for those with short attention spans

There are two reasons people like flowers that grow from bulbs: (1) they grow quickly in the spring to their full size and have big, showy flowers when our other stuff is just filling out its leaves; (2) you can't get bored with flowers from bulbs because, if the flower lives for more than a couple of days, something will come along and eat it – probably because it is the first available spring food.

Bulbs have to think it is winter before they will grow. This is why the stores are full of them in the autumn, in the expectation that you'll plant them right away. If you miss that window, it'll be a full year before that cycle comes round again. I once watched a man argue with a nursery owner about this. He was terribly red in the face at not being able to buy bulbs in the spring. He had seen all his neighbour's bright bands of flowers, and wanted a strip like that for himself. But there is only one time of year to think about a colourful bulb garden and that is from September to early November.

The marketers of bulbs know exactly what they're doing when they sell these bulbs to you, so you won't see any fancy text on the signs or labels. All you'll notice is the rack upon rack of photographs of bright, ruffled, textured and double varieties of daffodil, tulip, bluebell and hyacinth.

There is a temptation to plant one bulb per section of garden, but try them in a cluster for effect. Your nursery-person will tell you how deep to plant them, and this might be quite deep in colder regions where the soil freezes solid. Loosen the soil with a shovel, rake it flat, shove your bulbs in and cover the spot with a mulch of leaves. This will give them a bit of protection and may save them from becoming squirrel food.

When the flowers come up in spring, do all your appreciating fast – that'll be it for the year. Then let the greens die a slow and natural death. Tie them into a bundle if they insist on messy, floppy deaths on adjoining plants, or transplant them somewhere they can die in peace. Just don't cut away the leaves till they're good and yellow. The leaves are busy passing energy to the bulb, which is even now building next year's flower inside it. Give it a break, and a nice mulch, and your summer plants will soon grow over the spot.

covering for a chain-link fence, though. There are some variegated and ruffled varieties that aren't quite as blocky-looking as the typical one, so keep an eye open for the "fancies." Shake out the dead leaves with a broom now and then to freshen it up.

## Jasmine

I have my jasmines planted in the greenhouse, and they are trained out through a hole near the bottom and grow up fishnet and along the roofline. This protects their somewhat tender roots in cold winters but allows them lots of sun in summer. I don't get masses of flowers, but what I do get smells wonderful and the foliage is pretty and finely cut, unlike the big, bold hops and Virginia creeper leaves, and the less noticeable leaves of the honeysuckle.

## Virginia creeper

This is a strong, hardy vine that turns fabulous colours in the fall. It has the added advantage, as far as I'm concerned, of possibly being rather bald on the lower few feet, which allows you to plant all sorts of intriguing, bushy things in front of its base. I have seen Virginia creeper growing all over the place with absolutely no help from anyone at all, so try this one if you're nervous!

# EDIBLE LANDSCAPING

## 7

What is an edible landscape? Well, a landscape is
that area outside your window, and an edible
landscape is one you (or a furry or winged friend)
can eat. "Like my vegetable garden?" you ask.
Like a great big vegetable garden that reaches
from yard edge to yard edge, in which as many
plants as possible are not only good for food but
have other uses as well.

Let's pretend there has been a major earthquake, or that you just didn't make it to the grocery store after work. Let's also pretend that last year (smart thing!) you planted some edible landscape plants and now you can benefit from your wisdom and foresight. You can just march out and pick some salad greens from near the back door, perhaps some chard, green onions, lettuce, corn salad and chickweed. Perhaps you'll dig up some potatoes or Jerusalem artichokes from their permanent patch, pluck scarlet runner beans from against the carport, and bring in some apples for cobbler on the way back into the house. A snippet of lemon balm and peppermint will be nice to throw into the teapot after dinner. All of the above samples are hardy, easy to grow, and much more useful than a hydrangea.

The theory is that instead of planting merely pretty plants in your yard you replace your planting areas (and most of your lawn!) with something that will not only grace your dinner table but will also live on to produce again next year. The theory and practice of permaculture (permanent agriculture) and edible landscaping introduces lots of complex issues and arguments, but the supporting concept is simple (just like most of the complex issues of the world!).

Next time you have an opportunity to acquire a plant for the yard, think twice about your choice. Should you get a nice hydrangea, or a fall-bearing raspberry? Should a large fern fill out that corner, or a rhubarb plant? When Aunt Matty offers you a clump of daisies, point a trembling finger at the fine patch of sorrel of which she has too much.

## EXPAND YOUR HORIZONS

When you start dragging your plants home, remember that they don't need to go into your sunny veggie garden (that can now be saved for annuals like tomatoes and peas) but can be tucked in less obvious spots. Many of the perennial plants such as berry bushes and edible greens are much more tolerant of shade than annual vegetables, so they can be thrown into your gloomier corners. Start them off with some good compost and a soaking. Don't forget that if they don't do well after a year, it is a simple matter to try them in another spot.

While you're reconsidering your concept of where certain plants belong, start thinking multi-use in terms of each plant's novel characteristics. A prickly gooseberry can be planted where the dog tries to push through the fence to chase the next-door cat. A tree can be positioned to afford shade to your living quarters in the summer, break the winter winds, and perhaps provide nuts, fruit, a place to attach your bird and bat houses (and offer some privacy from the neighbours, as well). Jerusalem artichokes can be planted along an exposed length of fence to give you a fast-growing hedge for privacy in the summer, since they can grow eight feet tall. Your pea trellis can offer shade to your sitting area, and will keep the ground behind it cool for a patch of lettuce or mint. A sour-cherry tree may be so distracting to the local birds that they'll be too busy for your sweeter fare. Start thinking of rampant strawberries as ground cover and let them creep out of their given spot. They'll keep weeds down in otherwise unused spaces. If you're choosing a site for your potato patch, just pick where you want to put in another garden area next year and let the potatoes do the work of breaking the soil. Even if you're renting, you can start collecting plants and either keeping them in containers under trees or planting out the smaller ones such as herbs and edible greens.

This chapter is only a mini-primer of all the great, easily grown plants that folks should seek out for their gardens and drag around like old friends until they find a final resting place. Justice can't be done to the topic in a general book like this, but I hope to excite you with the possibilities so that you'll do more investigating on your own.

Check your local library for more details on permaculture, edible landscaping and forest gardening.

# THESE ARE A FEW OF MY FAVOURITE EDIBLE THINGS

## Corn salad

Who named all these crazy permaculture plants? Onions that are neither Welsh nor Japanese are named after both and now we have corn salad, which has nothing to do with corn and doesn't even resemble it. Whatever the name, corn salad is becoming a favourite. It's a tiny, lush plant, all of it edible, from which you can nip leaves all spring. Then it goes to seed and the next flush of plants arrives in early fall without a single gesture on your part. In spring, there they are again, dozens of the little blighters, for moving around or giving away. And corn salad doesn't get bitter as lettuce does. You might find these seeds listed under "mache" or "salad greens."

## Japanese bunching onions

My friend Diane, who eats her own salads almost year round on British Columbia's Sunshine Coast, introduced me to Japanese bunching onions (also known as Welsh bunching onions). These grow most of the year, dying down during heavy frost but coming up quickly in the spring. Just cut off green onion shoots as you need them and leave the plant to grow. You'll need quite a few plants in a patch if you use lots of green onion, but one seed packet will give you more than you will ever need, and you can take them with you when you move. An easy alternative to growing from seed is to cut one to two inches off the root end of the green onions you normally buy at the grocery store and just stick them, root down, in any soil. A Chinese friend told me this trick, and as a proud propagator I wondered why it had never occurred to me. The little blighters sprouted new greens and I paid them back by keeping them watered. You can plant them at any time of year when the ground is workable and get about another year out of them before they poop out, which they do seem to do. I also love my chives, planted just down the steps. I can duck out and snip a handful for salads or scrambled eggs.

## Kale

For a green you can just walk out and pick for a salad or stir-fry, kale is a good bet. Many of us have had bad experiences with kale, especially if we have folks from the Old Country who liked to cook everything to mush. But Red Russian kale is very sweet, especially after the first frost, as well as being darned good for you. A couple of decent plants will keep you in ready-to-eat red "greens" for many months of the year. Kale is another hardy, easy-care plant. Just pick leaves as you need them, and leave some for the mother plant to carry on.

## Lovage

While "love" would be too strong a word with regard to my lovage, I certainly hold it in high esteem. When I run out of celery, I can peel off a few leaves of lovage and chop them very finely into salad or soup to give me that celery flavour. Plant lovage in semi-shade, and it will come up relentlessly year after year. It tastes so strongly of celery, that you need very little and might even find that just rubbing the bowl gives enough taste and smell to convince the crowd. See chapter 5 for more ideas on incorporating herbs into your life.

## Perennial or sprouting broccoli

My friend Jess showed me her five-foot-tall purple sprouting broccoli and told me she and her husband had been picking from that one plant all winter. It was still very sweet and covered with little broccoli shoots in April. She finally cut it down because it was causing too much shade for her other veggies! Nine Star broccoli is good, too and don't forget to eat the leaves and flowers. A couple of these plants near the back door will keep you in soup greens, stir-fry bits and salad bits for months. Of course, regular broccoli with the single larger head is nice, but these fellows have a

different genetic agenda and will pump out lovely little tips for a much longer period of time. They also can produce for a couple of years.

## Tea plants

The plant leaf we normally consider "tea" is from a relative of the camellia, of all things. If you mix this leaf with *monarda*, or "bee balm," you get Earl Grey tea! This is where many of us stop, but the truth is that many plants in your garden will taste perfectly good tossed into the teapot. Try your mints, or some leaves from the bee balm. Lemon balm and lemon verbena give a nice scent. Garden sage, clover blossoms, strawberry leaves (and throw in a little wild strawberry) can be used, or camomile, lavender or raspberry leaves. These plants are all easy to grow and many will take over the yard if you let them. And — bonus — they all have other uses!

# BERRIES

There are hundreds of types of berries in the world. After all, berries are just a different vessel for seeds that birds and other critters can carry away from the mother plant to where the seeds won't compete for space and food. But something humans found out a long time ago is that some berries are much more worthwhile than others. Some are big and juicy and appeal to our desire for sweetness. These are the type of berries we've been dragging around the world with us, and here are some common North American varieties.

## Strawberries

Plant 'em. Eat 'em. The biggest challenge with strawberries is fighting off everything else that wants to eat them. You could hide little pots of beer under the mulch to catch slugs, and throw some loose netting on supports to keep the birds and other two-legged predators away. Strawberry plants will breed like rabbits, and then you can start giving them away or using them as ground cover under the back trees. Strawberries will be happy if you top-dress the plants, mulch them, and throw some manure tea at them now and then. You can start pretty quickly to feel like a successful plant breeder by snipping some of the spreading runners and giving them to friends. The runners you miss will grow into new strawberry plants, and when the "mother" gets exhausted-looking you can place her (gently, and with a kiss for all that hard work) in the compost heap.

## Berry bushes

Berry bushes come in two loose groups: brambles are the prickly, rambling things that look a bit like raspberry and include tayberry, youngberry, blackberry, loganberry and boysenberry; shrubs (currants, gooseberries, blueberries) tend not to have vicious thorns (except for the famous goose-berry) and can be trained into multiple forms. Care and feeding of both these types is the same — top-dress the soil around the main stem with aged manure and seaweed each spring, and put down a good layer of mulch such as hay, leaves or compost on top of that to smother weeds and keep the soil cool. Keep the mulch pulled away a few inches from direct contact with the stem so that nasties can't hide too conveniently. See chapter 8 for the very simplest of methods of keeping your berry bushes at bay!

Wild native berry plants — salal, Oregon grape, huckleberry, thimbleberry, salmonberry, wild strawberry — all are good for tucking into wild, shaded portions of your garden, and all the berries are edible.

## When good berries go bad

In some plant catalogues you will still see ads for — wait for it — "Tasty blackberries!" "Simple to grow!" Can you imagine paying money for a blackberry bush? It would be like buying rocks! Oh, never mind — I've paid for rocks. Anyway, here we were wondering if all those crazed

### Taming the berries

♦ The brambles (blackberry, raspberry, loganberry, tayberry, youngberry): These need lots of room to expand and a good trellis or wire system so that the prickles don't invade your paths

♦ The shrubs (blueberry, currants, gooseberry): These bushes can be trained to grow upright, or pruned to follow a fence

geneticists couldn't come up with something that would make the Himalayan blackberry just a little more susceptible to mildew, perhaps, or chicken pox, so that we'd have a lot more usable garden space. But the bad news is this: there is no good "sustainable" way to get rid of blackberries except for a full physical attack. You'll need sound shovels, pry bars, really good gloves, long sleeves, lots of excellent friends, many Band-Aids and several units of packed red cells.

You'll have to hack the visible parts of the plant back enough to get near the stump of the root where it comes out of the soil, and leave enough of that to get a good grip. You'll have to dig up the soil around each root enough to pull it out. This is horrible work but is much more satisfactory than just mowing the stuff each season, because in one weekend you can actually eradicate a patch for good and won't have to be waging the same war for years to come. Cut the canes and roots into smaller pieces to make them manageable, and then either run them through a chipper or leave them out to roast in the sun for a few days to make sure they're dead. Use the dead canes, with lots of shovelled-on soil, as landfill in some distant corner. If you have no room to do that, blackberries are one of the few items of plant matter I would haul away in a truck to the landfill, just because of the sheer bulk of them.

### Currant and gooseberry problems

Both these shrubs get by with minimal pruning, can take some shade, and come in a multitude of berry colours. However, they are victim to a horrible little green worm that must be handpicked all summer unless you want to use any of the organic sprays (garlic, chili, etc.), which are a real effort to apply front and back for the week after week that this worm persists. Don't be fooled by friends who tell you that non-organic sprays will solve your problem. My worms entered my yard on young plants from a non-organic nursery, which I'm sure is well treated with sprays, so it's reasonable to assume these worms have developed some immunity. My suggestion if you have a bad case of worms is to let the plants go and starve the little buggers out. Try again in a few years!

Whatever you do, don't rototill a patch of blackberry roots unless you intend to pick through the remains for every last piece of root and stem that might re-grow. One machine that would come in handy is a Bobcat, which can flip over big buckets of soil from which you can haul roots.

If you will miss your patch for pies and jam, one trick I've seen is to replant a healthy specimen in an old barrel but mow or cut away anything that grows down and hits the ground around the barrel, therefore keeping it "contained." If it gets out, run!

# FRUIT TREES

We usually think only of apple and pear, plum and peach when we think of fruit-bearing trees for the yard. Since we already have the fussy "domestic" trees in our yard, let's see what Bill is doing for his. Well, he's spraying them with something different throughout the year. He says it's for the bugs and diseases, but strangely enough, he still has the bugs and diseases. Since we know that the definition of insanity is to perform the same gesture over and over even though it doesn't work, let's try a new way of handling problems. Let's start with a healthy diet. If you had a friend who ate Twinkle Tops for breakfast, instant White Foam for lunch and numerous acid-flavoured drinks all day, it wouldn't surprise you if he had hemorrhoids, pimples and slightly unfocused eyes. So if your trees look like hell, why not give them the equivalent of multi-grains and veggies to eat? Try this method for a couple of years before you let Bill bother you any more. And give the guy a carrot, for God's sake.

First, if your trees are planted in the grass say goodbye to that grass by either weakening it with a thorough raking or applying a heavy layer of mulch. Yes, your fruit tree wants mulch, just like the rest of your plants! It would prefer it right up to the drip line, but partway will do. You can phone your local portable shredding service and ask it to drop off a load of chips, or a landscaping

## Trees with berries

These include the hawthorn, mulberry, serviceberry, Juneberry, and elderberry and other normally "wild" trees. No one has bothered to cultivate most of these because the berries are either too small for picking, not very sweet, or otherwise not worthy of attention. But the British used these trees in hedgerows as windbreaks and bird distractions, and still found ways to make the fruit edible. "Wild" trees tend to be happy when left alone to make their own way, so are excellent for the gardener who doesn't want to fuss.

## Nut trees

I have a quite complex book on the care of nut trees, but I also have various friends with hazelnuts, heartnuts and other walnuts and none of them do anything to their trees. Some friends are worried about their walnut tree, but are going to try a good mulch this year to see if they can excite it a little. Many nut trees will bear on their own, but apparently planting two or more gives them a choice of pollen and perks up the pollination rate. Never mind the details for now.

service that owns a shredder may want a convenient place to dump waste materials. Just make sure the company separates its material from unsprayed yards and saves it for you.

Next, spread manure, seaweed, ground shells, compost or anything else you would consider plant food all over the ground on your newly thinned grass. Cover this area thoroughly with chips, hay or straw, or leaves if it's wintertime. If it's summer, scatter your lawn clippings onto this layer to keep it thick. Leave a space around the trunk bare so that critters can't hide right up against the bark. If you have a peppermint or chive plant, chop away some roots and plant them around the trunk — I don't know why this works on bad bugs, but I haven't got any yet so it must do the trick.

# A KITCHEN GARDEN

I have a garden about four feet deep by eight feet long that runs along the wall of my little house to the corner. It contains the following plants:

- One mulberry tree, planted about one foot from the wall and intended to be trained upward in a fan shape to keep its shade at bay. It will be awkward to pick, except from the steps and the bedroom window, but it's out of the way and will take up very little garden space at the base
- One "super-duper" raspberry, which I imagine is super-duper only because it doesn't have to compete with other raspberry plants, or maybe because it likes its onion and strawberry companions. It is planted at the corner of the garden and is trained along the wall (behind the mulberry tree) and at my face level. I picked many berries off it last year. It was convenient for the times I just wanted a few berries for flavour or garnish
- One clump of green onions, so close to the bottom of the stairs that it's easy for me to run down and stick another rootlet in, and equally easy to cut shoots when I want them

❥ One Nine Star broccoli, which gives me one big leaf every other day to tear up into salads

❥ One kale plant, which gives me one or two leaves a day for stir-fries or salads

The ground under these plants is covered with strawberries to keep the weeds down and has cicely (salad leaves) and lemon balm (for tea) growing through it. I'm going to move a couple more salad plants into this bed, as well. The bed also has Peruvian lilies and other "pretties" in it, although it looks lush and green throughout the season and doesn't really need fancying up.

I weed this patch of garden each spring, give it manure tea, and re-mulch it with straw. That's about it, except for the odd watering and pulling of any really tenacious weeds that poke through. For a tiny area, it gives me a lot of tidbits for nine months of the year.

## And less stress, too

Besides the adaptability, the other thing I like about homemade permaculture gardens is the low-care casualness. If a lemon balm suddenly appears in the raspberries, or borage comes up with the potatoes, no problem! You can move them if you want, or just leave them be and let things grow where they thought they'd be happy. They know more than you do about some things.

Even the weeds have a place (as usual!). If you're scraping to save some dollars or just want an adventure, try some dandelion root as a coffee extender. A friend and I just about defoliated all of our friends' backyards, much to their delight, and none of our buddies ever guessed what was in the coffee. We just dug up dandelion plants from unsprayed yards, cut off and washed the roots, dehydrated them as much as we could outside on a tray, then cut them up eraser-size and put them in a low oven until they were leather-hard. Then we ground them up in the coffee grinder and threw handfuls in with the coffee. I hear chicory is good, too, and I love the flavour, but I am still struggling to grow the stuff.

## LAYERING SAVES SPACE

The nice thing about introducing these largely shade-tolerant, perennial edible plants to your yard is the fact that you can start "layering" your garden with useful things. I have strawberries growing under my raspberries, and I've trained my boysenberries along wires over my potato bed, which actually doesn't need full light, anyway. The dainty, shady medicinals like skullcap like being under the autumn olive bush, and things like cinnamon yam grow out of boxes along the pathways to save room. My nut trees are planted under the red elderberry, which is protecting them from harsh sunlight until they mature a bit and, meanwhile, I can hack mercilessly away at the elderberry to allow a bit more light through each year, without harming the bush. I have some mints and chokeberries planted around the little nut trees, because both will take the shade as the tree grows. Sweet woodruff is a really pretty little spreader, with tiny white flowers; it keeps the ground covered under my other shrubs and under the hops vine, which is quite shady. Woodruff is a medicinal, or useful if you drink a lot of mulled wine, and it keeps the ground cool and covered. Wild strawberries and miner's lettuce like shade, so are used for tucking underneath anything with a six-inch clearance. Layering is useful with grapes, kiwis and hops that would like the sun on them and can be used as a summer roof over the greenhouse or summer porch to keep out the worst heat.

In my "sunny" beds, I have camomile planted under the sage and will move my sun-tolerant thyme in front of it (since it's short, it won't block the sage's light), violets and feverfew in the shade of the lilies, and my sprawling rosemary at the foot of the jasmine and valerian. Behind that, the honeysuckle climbs up into the remaining sun and hides the wall of the house. In this way I can compress my planting areas, and they can make use of each other's size and density.

# THE EDIBLE CENTREPIECE

Potluck dinners make my skin crawl. I have to leave my garden, go into the kitchen, and worry about creating something that someone else will approve of. Blech! Much more in keeping with a gardener is the edible centrepiece, which is usually a novel enough offering to distract the host from the fact that you haven't actually brought any food.

Most summer dinners occur at a time when plants are wilting worst, so I pick my edibles earlier in the day and drop them right into a bucket of water. Then I can arrange them at my will and they'll be fresh and lush when everyone else is drooping. For a container, I find an old yogurt tub that will fit inside a terra cotta pot, but if I don't think the host will appreciate the sacrifice of the pot I wrap a plastic pot in fabric, or even use a crumpled paper bag with a gold ribbon. Then I cram the container with either that green foamy material that comes with gift plants (and can be used over and over) or use soil or packed moss to hold stems in place.

I begin the arrangement with full, short pieces of oregano and mint, then add a longer layer, of sorrel, beet leaves, basil, sage, garlic flowers, lemon balm, lovage leaves, rosemary cuttings, chive flowers, nasturtium flowers and leaves, calendula flowers and kale leaves. Next I add my accent pieces. Wonderful effects can be achieved with pinkish strawberry leaves (which can be thrown into the after-dinner teapot with the mint and lemon balm), dill and fennel flowers, *monarda* flowers, curly garlic tips and, if you can find strong enough stems, strawberry clumps on the stem. Guests love to taste and try to identify each plant, and are always amazed at the many scents the centrepiece gives off.

All these plant pieces should be picked in groups of three and carefully scanned for bug bites before you cut them.

There! And you didn't even have to cook!

## Garden dreams winter salad for the West Coast

(generously donated by Diane Nicholson, Queen of Winter Salads)

**Beg, buy or trade for seeds of any of the following:**

Arugula
Chervil
Cilantro
Collards
Corn salad
Cress
Endive
Gai lan (Chinese broccoli)
Giant Red mustard
Greenwave mustard
Johnny Jump-ups
Kales
Komatsuna (mustard spinach)
Lettuce (Arctic King or Winter Density)
Mizuna and mibuna
Pac (or bok) choy, etc.
Parsley
Spinach
Tendergreen mustard
Turnip greens

Mix some or all of the seeds listed in the left sidebar together with a little dry sand. Sow sparingly over a well-prepared and well-drained four-by-eight-foot bed in a sunny spot in August. Cover lightly with topsoil and firm it.

All of these seeds may be planted earlier or later with varying results (e.g., you may get some early bolting or small plant size), but this garden patch will still provide nutritious salad or sandwich greens every day in fall, winter and spring for at least two people. To extend your growing season, pinch off flowers and eat 'em! This will slow the process of your plants going to seed and dying down. This winter-garden method is admittedly unscientific and low-tech, but very easy. It can be accomplished in less than an hour, with daily watering until established.

One of the beauties of winter gardening is letting Mother Nature do the watering over winter; the other is laughing at the prices and often poor quality of the very expensive ordinary and gourmet greens in the stores. The fabulous flavour and health benefits of eating fresh greens in the winter are worth the small amount of work. Do this if it's the only gardening you do!

## I fed my mother weeds, and lived

My mom's nickname is "Sarge." I didn't think it would be easy to feed her weeds, especially in front of company from the city. Mom noted that I hadn't bought salad fixings to feed her friends, and I explained that I'd be picking them from the garden. She pointed out that I didn't have any lettuce in the garden. I told her we wouldn't be having any lettuce in the salad. She looked dubious. She has been fed "weird" things in the past.

Now, Dad and I are not picky eaters. We'd scrape berries off the sidewalk if necessary. But

Sarge is made of different stuff. Salad ingredients come from clean, well-lit metal bins at the grocery store. If they're proper food, that is.

Naturally, I had to drag Mom out to the yard for a reality-altering experience. Now, I knew better than to just stuff any old weed down my precious ma's throat. I'd have to tread carefully if I wanted to convert her. No strong arugula or fuzzy cicely leaves for her.

First, to throw her off, I harvested some silky beet tops and some very young pea pods. Then I picked a couple of leaves off the violets and nasturtiums along the path. She was still nodding. We reached the weed patch and I plucked some nice big tufts off the healthiest of the chickweed. Her eyebrows went up, but I kept picking. I showed her the Siberian miner's lettuce and pulled away the spent flowers (edible, but a bit stringy to the

---

### Edible flowers – an extremely compressed list of ideas

**Basil** – flowers good in tomato dishes

**Begonia** – dessert, garnish

**Borage** – candied, frozen into ice cubes for summer drinks

**Calendula** – edible and medicinal, used to colour eggs and rice, scattered into salad

**Chives** – salads, oil and vinegar

**Day lily** – (orange) chop into salads

**Dianthus** – herb butters, salads; remove white "heel" – it's bitter

**Dill** – salads, eggs, potatoes

**Geranium** – scented waters for jams and vinegars

**Hibiscus** – stuff with mango bits, eat fresh in salads

**Lavender** – vinegars, tonic waters

**Lemon verbena** – teas, to flavour jellies, ice cream, garnish

**Marigold** – see calendula

**Mint** – teas, desserts, bathwater

**Nasturtium** – salad, sandwiches

**Rose** – syrups and waters, pickle the rosebud, cook into fruit pies (remove white heel)

**Rosemary** – infusion for the face, put in salads

**Sage** – salads and teas

**Squash** – stuff with food mixtures, make into soup

**Viola** – good garnish, salads, ice cubes, fruit desserts

**Yucca** – remove bitter centre part; eat raw or cooked in salads or stir-fries

novice) to expose the little leaves. It's a bit tedious to pick, but it grows all year round in nice big clumps. Next I picked the big leaves off the corn salad, another plant that will re-seed itself once it's started. I picked my only remaining purslane, and a few leaves of wood sorrel and goosefoot. On the way back to the house I plucked a bit of kale here, a sorrel leaf there and a few young broccoli leaves. Now, just a dash of colour for my dear old mother's discerning eye: some *monarda* petals are truly wonderful, and a spent day lily flower, chopped finely, makes a faint burnt orange against the green. A bit of fennel, a touch of oregano, some perennial green onions and we were all set. There are more adventurous things to choose out there, but I didn't want to scare the little dickens ... I mean, Sarge.

Why was I feeding my mother weeds? She wondered, too. I explained to her that I didn't have to drive to the store as much now that I knew which plant parts I could eat from the garden. Not only was I saving fossil fuels for myself, but I was also avoiding supporting a delivery truck on the road, and the refrigeration costs. Plus, these garden greens are frequently higher in nutrients than their commercial siblings, and because they're picked fresh, they're even higher again than stored foods. And it's organic, man! Garden salad is free, because even the beet and broccoli leaves are just a byproduct of the veggie you're waiting for. And speaking of waiting — see any lineups in that yard? I don't think so!

Mom watched the tossing of all this crazy stuff with a detached eye. But she ate it all, as did the unsuspecting company. Mom gave me a sideways look and didn't tell them till the end that we were eating weeds. She looked quite pleased with herself. I think she's on to something. I wiped the sweat from my brow and headed off to get dessert. She looked afraid again. Goodness knows why.

# REFLECTIONS ON PRUNING

8

**WARNING! Advice in this chapter may cause apoplexy in the traditional pruner.**

Gardeners who are faint of heart are generally loath to study pruning techniques. Me too. Here are some general concepts you can live by until you are no longer faint of heart. This chapter was a terrible worry to get started. Was it because I decided to consult several pruning manuals, and they all disagreed with one another on the fine points? Was it because it's hard to make sweeping, easy statements when we're discussing pruning? Was it because I lack the pruning gene?

# IT'S A GUY THING

Heavy pruning is a guy thing, perhaps not genetic at all, but experientially acquired. The son watches his dad carefully as pater fires up the chain saw to remove a few unnecessary branches from a badly positioned bit of horticulture. Mom steps out onto the stoop with the dog bowl, sees the massacre in progress and screams, "YAAAACK! My prized *Oxydendrum arboreum*! I said just a little off the side!" And as she runs, wailing, back into the house, the dad looks balefully at his tender son, who nods knowingly, and the pruning gene makes its leap; the pesky generation gap has been breached once more. If you think this observation is sexist, please note that nearly all respected bonsai masters, topiary pruners and loggers are men.

On the other branch we have the nibblers, who wring their hands as they circle the intended victim, concern and doubt pushing at their brow, before they finally reach out and take the last four inches off a particularly inconvenient branch. Phew! Glad that's over. But you are going to assume after all this that I am going to suggest the middle path, and I am not.

# PRUNING CONCEPTS MADE EASY

Which brings us to item one, the disagreement among the pruning manuals. You see, tossing my own observations out the window, I was going to glean tidy rules of thumb for you — rules that you could absorb, experiment with and add to as the years went by. I was unsuccessful. The books were written by both men and women, traditional English gardeners and nouveau stylists, but heaven help them if they ever meet at a tea party. So I decided to give you the simple version (according to me) of why to prune, why not to prune, how to prune, and when to prune. You will receive pruning rules of thumb only for the plants I can explain easily; *don't touch the rest!* There! Simplicity is a wonderful thing.

# WHY PRUNE?

There are several reasons why you might want to prune a plant:

- Sometimes a car runs off the driveway and hits a shrub, resulting in a torn branch. Hmm, I suppose we should worry about the car, too, but ...
- Sometimes, you move into a new house to find that the surrounding shrubs have obviously been pruned by someone from the planet Zoron — while on drugs — in an electrical storm — while being swallowed by a snake — while being spoken to by a passing vacuum cleaner salesman. It's the only explanation. You can tell by the amount of haphazard growth that results
- Sometimes, probably because some human pruned them badly, shrubs and trees grow branches that overlap and rub on each other
- Sometimes, when certain growth is removed, the plant has more energy to create fruit that humans want to eat
- If you're trying to cram a lot of fruit-bearing life into a small yard, trees and bushes have to be shaped along fences and up posts to save space. This type of pruning is a bit fancy for these pages, but there are many books on the topic
- Sometimes you will want to chop back a tree or vine so that you can still reach the fruit

# WHY NOT PRUNE?

Pruning is not mandatory! All over the world, trees and bushes are producing very nice fruit without any intervention at all. But sometimes humans feel that nothing will happen properly without their sterling intervention, so they insist on pruning whether they know why they're doing it or not. Now that we've hit the 21st century, growers are experimenting with old beliefs and coming to the conclusion that Mother Nature might have been right all along. There are several reasons why pruning is not always the right choice:

- Most healthy plants, left to themselves, will develop a symmetrical, well-arranged system of growth that worked for their first billion years on the planet
- Plants have evolved with their own limits on how much growth they can manage per year, and chopping off bits makes them grow replacement parts on which they wouldn't normally have to waste energy
- Poor major pruning will require more professional help to correct than will small corrective work
- If you mess up the pruning, branches may cross, rub and die. The person who moves in after you will think you're from Zoron

Studies have shown that the yields of unpruned trees in total pounds are often higher than yields for pruned trees, but the fruit may be smaller and not as evenly coloured. Research by the Utah State Agricultural Extension showed that during the first five years of production the heaviest crops were on unpruned trees. (This sort of fruitfulness occurs only when the tree has sufficient water and soil fertility to sustain healthy growth.)

I tested that theory after scanning Masanobu Fukuoka's book *The Natural Method of Farming*. I had moved onto a property with several apple trees on it. After having a friend remove the tall, suckery growth from the very top of one tree, I left them all completely unsprayed, unfertilized, unwatered and unpruned for the seven years I lived on the property. Besides the pruning the bears did (Zoron-style, with vacuum cleaner salesman), the trees produced just as well as anything else in the area, yielding a tremendous bumper crop in my last year there. I also discovered an abandoned red currant bush on the property that bore huge amounts, again with no help from me, and to the great disgust of some naysayers. Other friends told me of visiting abandoned orchards every fall to pick the apples that grew prolifically there. So take your pick of the above reasons when you think you really must prune something.

# HOW TO PRUNE

Granted, the yard is more manageable when the dead growth is cut away and some plants do seem to appreciate a little pick-me-up now and then. Before you make any cuts, make sure you have sharp tools. No matter what tool you use, if the blade is dull it will tear the branch instead of cutting it. Once you have a sharp tool, sit in your lawn chair and look closely at a branch for a while.

You'll notice a few similar traits from one plant to another. All branches stick out at angles from a main stem or trunk. Arranged at intervals along the branch will be smaller branches, usually facing outward around the first branch. Out of that branch, even smaller branches are arranged, and so on. Look at large trees and small, young trees to see this pattern. Now: I am going to tell you what apical dominance is, and you're going to thrill others like yourself at parties for months to come.

The tip of each growing branch contains a chemical that represses growth at the other leaf buds farther down the branch. Call it greedy. Call it the head of the house. If you cut this tip off, the other buds will begin growing freely. Look at where the buds are pointing, and you will see where the new growth will occur when you cut off the tip of the branch. Cool, eh? A properly positioned cut would look like the cut shown in the sidebar diagram.

Of course, when you are removing dead branches you won't be worried about where the cut ends, because when you're cutting off dead tissue there is no growth to affect. But if you must make a live cut, whether for damage control or to make room for the kids to get down the walkway, look at where the last bud on the branch is pointing. If it's pointing somewhere awkward, cut back to a bud that is pointing where you want it.

## Some handy pruning tools

Knowing that good pruning shears are a bit expensive, I waited for my birthday to ask my

**A properly positioned cut**

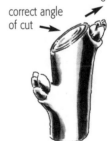

direction of new growth

correct angle of cut

family for this gift. They bought me a nice pair of what are called **anvil pruners**, good broad-duty shears that would handle most of the jobs I wanted done. I painted a fluorescent orange patch onto the sides and haven't lost them yet. The **bypass shears** are known to be generally lighter than the anvil type, good for small hands and good, close cuts, but may not have the same cutting power as the anvil types. Don't worry too much about those details right now, just get some good pruners!

Keeping the blade sharp is one of the tricky parts. You can also buy a handy little sharpening gadget that will help you keep just the right angle on your blade. Hmm, I should ask for one for Christmas. The next gift ... oops, I mean pruning tool on my list is **loppers**. These are giant pruning shears, much better suited to cutting back fruit trees and large shrubs than are your little ones. Some of the more expensive ones (and I would put this right onto your birthday list) are specially designed to turn your meagre little arm actions into decisive, mighty cuts. I can cut down a 20-foot alder tree with mine. Clean and oil the blades and hang them out of the muck, and you will have them for years.

## Tips for pruning specific plants

Here are some common garden food plants, and suggestions about what to cut off them.

**Fruit trees**
My friend Eric (a guy) is a master at pruning his fruit trees. They are gorgeous and symmetrical and grow where he wants them to grow. We are not masters. Stick with these basics.

Cut out the sappy "whips" that sometimes grow out of the top of fruit trees like a bad haircut. These are (naturally) the result of last year's pruning and don't seem to occur on unpruned trees. Also cut out the thousands of tiny stems that grow out around the base of the tree. They will grow back. Cut them out again.

Although pruning guides may tell you to cut out branches that grow and droop heavily to one

**Healthy blades**
You can help the blades of your pruner stay in good shape by not twisting them during a cut, by not cutting over-large branches, and by not sticking them into the gritty soil to cut roots.

side, I will point out that the hangy-down branches are noted for high fruit production (because of some hormone that gathers there) and if you just leave them you will see for yourself. Prop them up with some stakes so they don't break, and pick all that great fruit. If a fruit tree is just bulging with young fruit, don't hesitate to pinch out any that seem misshapen or bruised. This will allow the others around them to grow better. You might want to intentionally pinch out a few tiny apples or peaches if they look too close together. Of course, left to itself, the tree will drop fruit it can't support so you don't really have to follow that step, either.

### Raspberries

As soon as the last fruit is picked, that particular stem will begin to die. Cut it back to the ground. New green shoots will have appeared and grown around this one. They will bear fruit next year. Some people cut them back to a five-foot stem in fall so that they don't straggle and snap in the winter.

### Brambles

Cut out the weak-looking branches of blackberry and loganberry after they have fruited. Leave them if they look strong; you may get another year of fruit out of them. Before you get nervous about pruning your brambles, remember those blackberries that you hack at wildly each summer to reach the fruit? And how prolific and thickly they grow after that kind of massacre? Right! Don't sweat when you cut back brambles.

### Grapevines

The numerous methods and terminologies for cutting back grapevines would scare even a courageous gardener. After reading more than 15 methods, I suggest the following rule of thumb: cut the main vine back to about eight feet in winter, and prune each branch from the vine back to the second leaf bud. I will await the many letters from vine growers who will give me heck for that, but on the other hand I bet none of your grapevines will die if treated this way.

## WHEN TO PRUNE

Shrubs and trees sometimes may look inactive, but those cells inside are actually monitoring growth, racing nutrients around and keeping the water situation under control. When you remove a branch, the alarm sounds and the cells must make some hasty decisions. Should the cut be healed? Should new growth go there, perhaps a nice new branch? Since plants need a certain amount of green top to collect the sun's rays, and roots to collect water and nutrients, removing chunks of either of these throws the balance off briefly. The plant wants balance and will replace what it needs to support its bulk and age. (Hmm, if this worked for humans it would mean that after every haircut we would all get to eat a nice big piece of cheesecake. Wouldn't it?)

Back to that cut you just made. If you hacked back your precious hedge or fruit tree in late summer, the plant in question would quickly pump out some new branches to even things out. But soon winter would come, and those tender bits of new growth might be too thin-skinned to survive. The leaves they created so prettily and with so much energy would just fall off in winter, before they got to do any good. So it would be a lot of work for nothing, wouldn't it?

This is why most plants are shaped in the spring, when the roots are busy sucking up nutrients, new growth will have time to be of benefit, and fresh green wood has time to harden before next winter.

Trees, especially fruit trees, are pruned in winter or *very* early spring, when they are fully asleep and their sap is not running. The resulting big, open wounds aren't as exposed to all those diseases and "rots" that occur in warm weather and the sap won't be flowing out of the wound. The tree will "come to" in the spring and its cells will have to rearrange how they were going to do things, now that all the tips have been cut away.

### Final observations

Obviously, when a tree or plant gets accidentally damaged outside the normal "pruning season" it doesn't mean it will die. It just means the plant will have to work hard to make changes that may not be of huge benefit to it. That's my observation on it, but then, I'm not from Zoron.

# PESTS – TO SHARE OR NOT TO SHARE

9

We tend to think that our world was an empty landscape until, ta-dah, humans appeared and cleared the land, built a dream home and put in a septic system and a barbecue pit. What we forget is that the building lot had teemed with active, hungry critters for thousands of years but they all got pushed to the side, along with the local flora they had been munching on, by the bulldozer that put in the septic system. No one really noticed where they all went.

In the next step in human development, we planted tasty, luscious stuff where those blechy, overly chewy forest foods used to be and we wondered why, why, why all those critters suddenly appeared back in our gardens, looking a little more chipper. Survivors aren't stupid, and you could just hear them all muttering in their various critter languages: "Strawberries? Lettuce? Hey! Let's say we *adapt our diets*!" And the humans cried out in surprise: "ARRGGH! Slugs! Birds! Bears! Deer! Mice! Raccoons!" And the forest critters rued the loss of their ancestral home and all that food they used to eat that was *right there* but what the hey, this new stuff wasn't half bad if you kept the goofy humans at bay.

You can see where the conflict arises, and you should just be happy that the critters don't picket. The above is intended to make the reader a tad more sympathetic to other animals, and to suggest the possibility of sharing our wealth, or at least a wee bit of it. Here are some hints on sharing, as well as ways to not share your garden bounty.

## ON SHARING

If you own your lot, or know you'll be there a long time, make sure you leave and protect an area where your local wild flora such as salal, Oregon grape, elderberry and milkweed may grow. The local wildlife recognize this stuff and may prefer it to your garden. Leave a good patch, as much as you can spare, and let it grow wild. If a nearby building lot is being cleared, get in there ahead of time and dig up some of the plant life to return to your garden. Some people are concerned that bringing native food plants so close to the garden will promote fruit-stealing, because now the birds will be nesting right on the property and will only have to flutter across the yard for a little takeout. But if there is just a bit more for everybody, the competition for your tasty fruit won't be as fierce, will it? These wild areas also supply a resting zone for migrating birds and insects that prefer to rest and feed in familiar settings and you'll be helping the planet out, as well. As you can see, expanding your wild area is a benefit all round.

Another method for sharing with hungry critters is something called the rabbit garden — a patch of garden planted outside the guarded radius, free for the rabbits to munch on so they won't have to make the long hop all the way to your veggies. This can work for other species, too.

Someone with lots of space could set up bird stations in a clearing far away from the garden, and let everybody fight over the seeds and fruit in the feeder, leaving the garden relatively unmolested. Consider whether a gimmick like this has any place in your approach to the problem. Sharing might also include planting extra seed, with the full expectation that you will end up with only part of your crop.

I know many people who feel strongly that you can wish and will animals away. For those with the patience to try, please do. This is a peaceful technique, and I have had it work with bears. I made a silent bargain that they could eat all the "backyard" apples they wanted as long as they left the front-yard tree to me. Even though they surrounded the front-yard tree with large bucketsful of bear poo, in seven years they never climbed it or ate the fruit, so maybe there is something to say for this method. However, I have not had it work with anything smaller than a bear. This is the fly in the ointment.

On a not-so-peaceful note, after observing animal behaviour I am quite aware that humans are the only critters that call the family and take pictures as the local wildlife tears their garden apart. No self-respecting four-legged type would ever put up with a stranger wandering in and eating their dinner. For this reason, I have become more confident about screeching and snarling (like a good little raccoon) to defend my dinner-to-be. So the following section is on not sharing.

# ON NOT SHARING

## Slugs

On the wild wet coast, these slimy things have got to be the worst problem we will encounter besides bears. And deer. And mice. And Bill.

### The barrier method of slug control

Slugs have tender tummies and this fact can be used against them. You can circle individual plants or garden plots with wood ash, crushed eggshells, crushed seashells and sand. You can nail copper bands around the garden boxes, or nail thin strips of fine window mesh along the tops of the boxes to scratch their bellies. Ouch!

### The insidious trap method

Set up stations containing food much more yummy than a slug could ever expect from your garden. They seem to like the smell of crushed vegetation, so scrunch up your bitten lettuce leaves and push them into a ball on the path, and catch the slugs when they come to it. Or push into the soil cat-food tins filled with beer or yeast and sugar mixed with water, and let them crawl in and drown. My friend's new method is to grate some potato around the edges of flattened cardboard. They will come and eat the potato, and go under the cardboard to sleep it off.

### Snakes and slugs

Get over your fear of snakes. They keep down slugs — as do ducks, but ducks are harder to house than snakes. Snakes are also quieter, don't eat your lettuce, and won't leave poop all over the front porch when they want attention.

### The hunt-and-poke method

Slugs like being cool and they like the dark, so dawn and dusk are prime times to get out and hunt down the little horrors while they're travelling to and fro. It may seem that an unending supply of slugs keep appearing but if you are diligent, even for two weeks in the spring, you can make a big dent in the population. It'll be worth it to you all summer to work hard in the beginning.

### Getting rid of the evidence

Obviously, the fewer slugs you have around your garden the better. If you have an aversion to killing, drop all those bodies into a container and take them far away from the garden. The books say that slugs don't have a huge range, but I think you could attach a radio collar to some of mine and follow them by helicopter.

For the less squeamish, a good poking or cutting tool can be used to make the death as quick and merciful as possible. A friend uses scissors to cut them in half, but even I can't bear the thought of cleaning up after that rampage. Some people shake salt on them to kill them, but this is a slow and horrible death (some people don't care). Some poke the slug as hard as they can, then fling it into a saltwater mixture to ensure its death. This makes driving them to the park have some appeal. Whichever method you choose, remember that for every slug you get rid of now dozens more aren't born.

## Bears

It may surprise you to find "bears" listed *after* "slugs" in the pest section, but heck, bears aren't such a constant hazard for the garden. They're more seasonal, more regional, and can't hide in the pansies as well. You will never find a bear stuck to the bottom of your shoe.

When they do hit, though, it's a doozy. A bear can strip the branches off an apple tree, rip your shed apart for the blood meal, drink all your fish fertilizer and still be hungry for more. Apart from erecting an electric fence, there's little you can do to protect your garden from a stubborn bear. Fall seems to be the most important time for bears to eat — like us, they need to add a fat layer for winter. Knowing this, you can harvest apples, corn and nuts as soon as you can bear (!) to do it. You may have to clean up the garden as soon as you hear of bear warnings. Look up recipes for drying, ripening and freezing your stock a bit early. Never let rotten fruit sit on the ground — bears can smell that a mile away.

Don't let your local bear get complacent about using your yard as a restaurant. Whenever you can safely do so, bang pots and yell from a distance. Make "your" restaurant an annoying one to visit. One important note: never approach a feeding bear. They're at their nastiest right about then. Your local conservation officer may be able to help with more tips, and as a very last resort might come and trap it and take it to someone else's backyard to eat fruit.

## Raccoons

Good fences are expensive, and few of them work for raccoons. I can offer only a few suggestions. First and foremost, never feed a raccoon on purpose. If your intention is to feed yourself from your own yard, it is best to establish a clear relationship right away. Since you are much larger than a raccoon, I suggest what might work is your clear declaration that "this is mine. Get your own, Bob." Raccoons can truly trash a garden, just like a bear. They're smart critters and will find somewhere else to eat, which is why they aren't endangered, so don't worry about them and don't start off on the wrong foot.

There are some fence designs that are effective for raccoons, but they are a bit of an investment. Electric fencing is effective and not quite as costly. Some readers will prefer not to use electric fencing and instead should try aversion therapy. The proper response on seeing a raccoon in the yard is to scream and shriek (even if the beast is just standing innocently on the driveway), throw empty plant pots, or turn on the hose and make sure that critter starts to run. Keep your distance, and make sure you leave a clear path of escape. Leave some piles of ammo near the door for convenient launching. Empty pop or beer cans with a bit of gravel in them make a great noise on impact, are recyclable, but won't hurt the raccoon. Once it's running, keep up a distant, convincing racket until it's got a good adrenalin rush. This will improve its memory. Try this for a while

— it may be worth the trouble. If this doesn't work, phone your local conservation officer to get more details on live trapping.

## Oh, deer

It's really hard to throw a tin can at a deer because deer are so darn lovely and vulnerable-looking — those big, brown eyes are a killer. It's also expensive to fence a whole property. However, to my own surprise, I would suggest the raccoon treatment on deer as well. Oh, no swearing, of course, and throwing plant pots would be very undignified. But certainly a good shouting won't damage their little souls for long. I let Cooma bark at them and that scares them away, but I have never encouraged her to give chase. I certainly have tried running a line of human urine (from a bucket, silly — the other way is a guy thing) along their usual route with, I believe, some success. It makes me think that just before the beans are ripe this year I should have a small garden party (with lots of beer). Some new blood-meal products are earning good reports, and I saw a bottle of coyote urine in the local nursery last week. Didn't say how they got the coyotes to urinate in that bottle, though.

I have heard lots of good things about horizontal fencing, which involves laying wire fence on the surrounding lawn so that the deer have to step onto the fence strands and will feel too uncomfortable to proceed. Then there's fishnet (with ribbons or cedar boughs woven in so that animals don't crash into it in the dark), electric fencing and double fencing. And then there's buying an alfalfa bale and a salt lick and setting it down near the creek and hoping for the best.

## Birds in the bush

Birds sure do have the advantage. They can sit on a branch and look at you for a long time, then swoop down and peck a big hole in that strawberry you've been guarding for two days. Tooth-gnashing is lost on them. They can't relate!

### Raccoons and the improved gene pool — a true story

The day I put my 13 new goldfish in my pond, I had my first (and, so far, only) raccoon visit. When I heard Cooma barking, I ran to the door and did my complete screaming meemies routine. This is quite an interesting show. At the morning count I was down to three fish but, boy, they sure were fast swimmers! This is a true tale of survival of the fittest, because I never lost another fish to raccoons and the only ones left to breed must have been the brightest and quickest of them. Sometimes you just have to give in to the grand scheme.

Used netting, floating row cover (check your garden store), old sheer living room curtains or any item like this can be thrown over small portions of the garden, but in big areas it may be worthwhile buying some old fishnet. Fake owls work for a while, but have to be moved. Once you have the birds where you want them, you can return to a shared garden by making sure there is plenty of elderberry and cotoneaster, salmonberry and thimbleberry, perhaps even a pin cherry tree. This will keep them amused and leave lots more for you, since your fruit is now not the only game in town. Birds like red, so plant lots of red berry trees (like elderberry and mountain ash) in the nether reaches of the garden.

## Aphids

Aphids look like a swarm of grey or black fuzz on the leaves of your plants, but on close inspection you'll see it is covered in tiny legs. Most plants can manage a few aphids, and if you see quite a number developing on a particular plant it probably means that something was already slightly amiss with the plant. Some people find, for instance that one broccoli plant will be infested with aphids while the rest are relatively free of them. You may start seeing the value of leaving them on this particular plant (call it your sacrificial broccoli). If they do begin spreading to surrounding plants, consider pulling up the whole offending plant and taking it to the edge of the yard, where frogs and other critters can have a good feed. You may want to put it in your "poo tea" bucket with a plate over it (play *Titanic* music as they drown). If your infestation is not serious, just keep the offenders too tired to eat by hosing them to the ground with a strong burst, keeping your hand under individual leaves to prevent them from tearing from the force of the water. Heavily infested leaves can be removed individually. Aphids aren't a problem in small numbers, so just keep hosing them until they are *in* small numbers. Repeated infestations are a sign that something is out of whack in your garden. Time to try Activity #1 in chapter 15.

## Sawflies and cabbage loopers

Some snazzy, full-colour gardening books have pages of photos identifying all of the annoying insects that may damage your plants, and the good ones that are helping your plants. I would like to simplify the whole process quite drastically.

What should you do if you find a bug eating your plant? Why, stop it, of course! Duh! First you have to be able to see it. Upon careful inspection, you may find a small leaf-coloured caterpillar lying just along the vein of the leaf. Then you'll see another, and another, and your life will be changed forever. (You may have to trust me on this one.) You'll want to get a cup or jar and poke that little caterpillary thing into it, where it will roll up and fake death. It's lying, so don't be fooled. Make a careful check around chewed leaves for more and take your time to check all leaves, top and bottom. You will have to do this again next week, so the more you catch today, the better. Also look for tiny white cones stuck to the leaves, because these are the eggs of the worms. Pick them off. When you have a cup of these things, you have another tricky decision to make. Feed 'em to the chickens? Drown 'em? Squish 'em into green soup under your gumbooted heel? Don't feel too bad about killing them. They're hell to rehabilitate, and remember, they lie. I know. I've tried to believe them.

### The good, the bad, and the bug-ly

Good bug ... or bad bug? If it's eating your plant, it's a bad bug. If it's eating a bug that's eating your plant, it's a good bug. That's all you really have to know, although I would never steer a truly interested bug fan away from a good identification manual at the used-book store. This is actually a good idea at some point because you won't, for instance, want to kill a baby ladybug (which is a lumpy, unappealing thing for quite a long time). The dead giveaway is that it will not be eating your plant — just the things that eat your plant.

## ON PATIENCE AND SUPPORT

I hate to go into too much detail about what can go wrong, bugwise, in a garden, because things going wrong is actually (1) a message and (2) a transient state, on the way to things going right.

Disease and bug infestation normally occur when something is wrong with the soil or the plant is genetically weak. If you have problems, sit in your lawn chair and think of what could need shifting. Are things getting a bit stressed because they aren't watered enough? Should you be giving plants a good shake of wood ash when it rains, to keep the pH at a proper level? Run through your list, and be patient while waiting for change.

If you take over gardens that have been gardened "hard," with overuse of nitrogen fertilizers, or application of pesticides that may have removed important "good" bugs, it will take a while to get the balance right again. Resign yourself to helping this one patch of earth through the transition. Feed it slowly but continuously. Let all its bug life return to an even keel by not being overzealous about what is allowed to live in your garden. Remember that you want "good" bugs to live in your yard, and they won't unless there is the chance of finding the odd "bad" bug to eat. So go easy, and let your garden be a lush, living space.

# CONTAINER-GARDENING

## 10

Container-gardening is a term that covers everything from tending a small lettuce in a teacup on the porch to nursing a whole "movable feast" of pots and bathtubs, old paint cans and boxes on wheels, containing anything that will live with a restricted root system. This is a great method for the transient gardener or for someone wanting to expand their growing area onto a deck or rocky corner.

Most plants, and even small trees, will survive quite happily in a pot of some kind, but I admit this form of gardening is reserved for someone with a dedicated watering gene. Container plants can't dive for their own water, so they tend to dry out quickly, especially with hot, dry air surrounding the pot. These plants need soaking every single day in the summer, so there is no point starting this method of gardening unless you know you'll water them well.

If you do decide to commit yourself to the extra watering, you are entering a very exciting gardening form. Berry bushes and small fruit trees, lettuce, roses and strawberries, sorrel and herbs, orange trees and ivy are all more than happy to live in a container that's in any condition, as long as it stays moist and they get a good splash of manure tea now and again. And they like to live in combination, too so if you have a spindly bottomed raspberry in a pot, plant nasturtiums, sorrel or strawberries to fill out the base and protect the soil from the sun.

**Have plant, will travel**
The beauty of container-gardening is the pleasure of bringing a flowering plant to the deck to admire and being able to put it back in the shade when the flowers die down. Pots can be shuffled around according to the plant's needs, something you can't do as easily in the average garden.

## REGULAR MAINTENANCE

There are a few methods for keeping your potted plants happy. The main trick is to keep them out of direct sunlight. Setting them under bushes or trees, or behind a lattice or screen, will keep the soil in the pot cooler. If you must leave them in the sun, try propping up a large board in front of the row of pots to create some shade, or make a decorative sun guard for the pots to hide behind while the plants stand free. Plant pots that are on the east or west side of the house will have only a half day of extreme heat, so try placing some there. If a plant seems to be scorching (as evidenced by faded, dry-edged leaves), give it a soak and move it to a shadier area. Cut away the burned parts of the leaf and watch it for further damage. You'll get to know which plants burn easiest, and will probably find that the more shade, the better.

# YEARLY MAINTENANCE

If you really want to keep your container plants healthy, once a year put aside a morning for upkeep. Sift some compost into a wheelbarrow and take it to a spot near the hose. Gently shake each plant out of its container, and if there is very little soil left in the pot look for a larger one. Place some of the compost into the pot, reset the plant into it, and push compost all around the top to even it out. Give the plant a good soaking before returning it to its spot. It will still be happy to receive a monthly dose of poo tea, but the compost will give it a boost. Some plants are happy in the same pots for years, but will appreciate having the old soil shaken off and compost added in its place.

If a pot is too heavy to lift, scrape all the soil you can from its surface (use your fingers so you can avoid damaging roots) and replace it with compost. The compost is likely to sprout seedlings all over the soil surface, but a mulch of moss or hay will keep them strangled. You may get a surprise, though. Your container garden may start producing young tomato plants, or borage seedlings! Leave them in if they look interesting. They can't hurt anything, and if you feed them they just might produce.

While you're transplanting, pick off dead leaves, trim away dead branches and give the foliage a nice bath to freshen it. Then soak the soil with the hose, and if the soil sinks down and exposes the plant's roots give it another handful to re-cover them. Replace your moss or wood chips.

As plants grow (or, ahem, die) they'll need readjusting within their groups. Obviously, tall plants should go toward the back of a grouping, shorter and fuller ones out front, but don't make a straight line if you can avoid it. Try to reproduce a natural combination of leaves and textures when you move your containers around. Lift some up onto wooden rounds or blocks for a change of height. Set some garden art amongst them for some contrast.

### Tricks for keeping them moist and cool

Mulch the top of the pots with gravel, moss or straw to reduce dehydration. You can also try double potting: place a small pot in a larger one, and stuff the outer pot with moss or straw to absorb heat. Another must in container-gardening is to leave plenty of room at the top of the pot for water to pool and then soak into the soil, rather than run over the sides too quickly.

# TYPES OF PLANTS

The easiest way to tell which plants will do best in a container is to visit a nursery. You'll see young evergreen trees and rhododendrons, rose bushes and grasses. You'll notice that a lot of the annual flowers, which grow quite quickly in one season, don't look too keen on the idea of living in those little pots, and that's because the nursery can't afford to plant them all into bigger ones. But you can, so try taking note of what looks as if it is strangling, offer the nursery a deal, and take the kid home for a bigger pot. Check out friends' choices, too, to see what looks effective.

Some plants that do poorly in pots are tall, spindly things such as cosmos, which are easy to grow but fall over when planted in small numbers in a pot. Lilies do fine; irises, the herbs, and even young fruit and nut trees can spend two or three years in a big pot before they begin to fret.

It's nice to have a few evergreen pots on your porch, and some ivy, periwinkle and ferns will stay happy all winter, but I don't want to start sounding like Martha Stewart.

# THE FINER POINTS OF CONTAINERHOOD

There is no limit to what a container should look like (ask Martha!), so making some for yourself is a satisfying project. The main goals for an effective container are that: it will retain moist soil all through a hot day (which means the bigger the better), it is deep enough to hold some mulch around the top, water can drain out of the bottom, and it is not too awkward to move around easily.

A friend made a big terra cotta pot with a really spiky exterior. It looked very wild, but once it was full of soil it couldn't be picked up without piercing the mover's hands. This is an example of *bad* design! Dangerous spikes aside, if you have a drill, or even a hammer and a large nail, you can make holes in the bottoms of lots of found items to make plant containers. If you have a pile

**Sounding like Martha Stewart (and she hasn't even thought of this yet)**

You can plant bog and water plants like arrowroot and lily, taro, butterbur and cyperus on the porch, in pots with no holes (naturally!). A lot of these plants are so dramatic-looking, and so easy to look after since they hold water longer than your other pots, that I will give myself some credit for starting what I hope will be a major trend. When planting water plants, I still top off the soil with gravel. It looks cleaner, keeps the weeds down, and I can tell at a glance when the gravel is dry that I have to refill the pots. Use any good garden soil with compost in these pots.

of discarded wood, try inventing some window boxes for your deck. Once the foliage starts spilling over the sides, no one will notice a few mistakes. Driftwood can be effective with plants tucked into it, but I hear it needs to be left in the rain a while to wash away some of the salt. Wood-furniture stores often have "matching" wood scraps that can be nailed together in some way or other. Just remember to connect the walls well enough to support the weight of all that wet dirt you'll be piling into it, and make the drainage holes *first*, if you have the chance, since some designs might make this awkward later. This should be the first thing they remind you about in pottery class, from the looks of all those planters that (1) won't hold a commercial plant pot inside and (2) won't drain water when they have something planted directly inside them.

Watch the weight if you're making a big item, or move the container into position before filling it with soil. Make sure it can withstand the elements. If you're painting a container, try to visualize what you'll be planting inside it so that you can enhance it with your colour choices. Play with texture and contrast when you're planting your containers, or choose the same plants for several. There's no end to what the human mind can contrive, so go "get wild" and just remember to keep up that watering.

## And they have it in your colour!

"If it holds soil, it must be a plant pot." This is what my wildly creative friends seem to be saying. Paul makes wire forms, packs them with moss and hides the plant pot in the centre with the plant spewing out like a volcano. Diane plants ferns in her moss baskets and nails them onto old posts — "hardy palm trees," she calls them. I've seen coffee cans painted all the same, trailing down a staircase, bursting with geraniums. Ada ran out of bonsai pots, so she's using roasting pans and carefully hiding that fact behind her fuller, lower plants on her deck. Alannah has torn the paper label off an empty paint can, created her own designs on the silver finish and slipped a plant into her new container. I like appliances, myself. I used to have an old-fashioned toilet out on the porch with a healthy mass of green creeping out of it. Now I have a sunken bathtub, the same mocha colour as my home (matching appliances, so necessary in today's modern world), filled with soil and water and holding my arrowhead tubers. I tried to get an old wood stove to train ivy through, but the owners got smart when I showed some interest in it. They're keeping it!

Smaller found items include clean hubcaps, old pails and leaky watering cans and large plastic food containers. Metal coffeepots are easy to drill holes into. China teapots can be used if you put lots of rocks in the bottom, and then pour excess water out of the spout! Big seashells, wooden salad bowls, old gumboots, wooden chairs with the seats cut out ... Hey! Where are you going with my slippers?

# GREENHOUSE CONCEPTS

## 11

Greenhouses are among those items that stand high on the wish list but, once possessed, seem to lose their charm. There are lots of predictable reasons for this, most of them circling around a basic misunderstanding of what a greenhouse needs from you to do its work. The rest of the reasons lean toward the human tendency to lose interest after the first flush or the first set of failures.

## WHAT IS A GREENHOUSE?

Any block of space that is protected from the elements by a clear or semi-opaque substance acts as a greenhouse. This can be a huge, glass addition with automatic vents, a simple two-by-four-inch frame leaning against a south wall with clear plastic stapled to it, or something that's as ornate as a whimsical carpenter with a bunch of old windows and oodles of talent can assemble. Although the person owning the more expensive version will tell you that his or hers is better, and in fact to die for, the real difference lies in how many healthy plants are actually growing inside. An eager gardener can win that contest hands down with a little enthusiasm and about two key pieces of information under her belt.

## TYPES OF GREENHOUSES, IN A NUTSHELL

The **cold** greenhouse is one that receives no heat during the winter. It is generally used in summer to boost seedling growth and protect houseplants and cuttings. The **hothouse** receives controlled heat, perhaps electric, gas or solar, so that orchids and taro and other exotics can be grown year round. You know you have died and gone to heaven when you have one of the latter. Either that, or you haven't opened a utility bill for some time. But even with an electric heater sitting on a ladder you can ripen oranges and lemons in Canada, so the thrill of bill-opening may be worth it.

The term **passive solar** greenhouse describes one that is designed to absorb the sun's heat and use no other power. For example, the building could be twice as long as it is deep, to take advantage of that low winter sun, with a low grade to the roof and the back wall coated with heat-retaining material and covered with something that reflects light. With no outside heat, this should keep your greens going all winter.

The **portable cold frame** is a wooden box used for keeping maturing seedlings out of the cold spring wind. They can be made out of scrap wood, and the glass top can be an old window or a used shower door. Some cold frames are small enough to be carried around as each patch gets seeded, giving the seedlings a quick boost of protected environment in which to grow. This item is definitely next on my list.

**Plant caps** are small glass or plastic containers (for example, plastic milk containers with the bottom cut out) that you pop over your new seedling in the spring. If you pile up the soil around it so that no critter can slither underneath, you'll be able to see differences in the way the protected plants grow next to their uncovered siblings.

# THINGS TO THINK ABOUT WHEN PLACING YOUR GREENHOUSE

You don't have to stop at one greenhouse — put them all over the place! One for morning sun, one for afternoon. You can have a lean-to for the tomatoes, a cold frame near the gate, and still build a room-size addition onto the house. Having too much greenhouse space is like having too much money, or too much time, as far as I'm concerned. And if you aren't using your extra space right now, you'll still have it in the future.

## Light

Right, you will need sun, especially spring and fall sun, to hit your new building. If you only have a choice of capturing morning sun or late-afternoon sun, keep in mind that afternoon sun in summer will create an amazing amount of heat, and probably more light than your plants need.

## Proximity

The closer to your house, the better, because you will run out there in your slippers to do a quick before-work watering, and pick some cutworms off the young broccoli, if you think you can do it before the baby wakes up/the boss phones/the cat licks all the butter off your toast.

## Water

Having access to a hose will make or break your summer crop. It's easy to say that you'll be happy to use a watering can, but you'll be using a lot of water in midsummer and you will have to be very dedicated to keep all the plants hydrated all day.

# WHAT DOES A GREENHOUSE DO?

We know that plants need light and water, but they also like some heat to get blasting in the spring. Seeds sprout only when they reach a particular temperature in the spring and, for many of the vegetables and annuals, that is more likely to be a late-spring temperature than an early one. The greenhouse will extend your spring by permitting those seeds to sprout in the nice warm air that was captured by your walls and dirt floor. It will also extend your fall season, as you'll find that certain plants will live quite happily with the protection from thick ice and wind chill, or at least will sprout out earlier in the spring.

I read somewhere years ago, and filed away in my head, that the main purpose of a greenhouse is not to provide higher heat but to moderate the day/night (or hot/cold) swing every day, so a greenhouse built directly onto the soil, or that contains water bottles for a heat sink, will be endlessly more helpful than one on legs, for instance, that has no way to retain heat at night. Think of this as your design.

The greenhouse will protect your young plants from getting eaten by pests. If pests do find their way in you have a good chance of finding them and clearing them out and having a bit of peace before the next batch stumbles upon the open door (they haven't seen the blueprints). The door will keep cats and dogs from visiting that new bathroom they think you've built them, and you can lean a small half door across the bottom to keep out these bigger pests when you want that extra ventilation in the summer. You can store your "tricky" plants in the greenhouse in winter because you know it will not be *as* cold for *as* long, and because there is no constant rain or snow melt things like rosemary and lavender won't rot. Loquats won't snap from snow damage, and those hardy palms won't rot at their core.

## The bad stuff

Greenhouses get really, really hot in the summer. We know that plants can take a lot of heat if they have sufficient water to keep their little cells wet, which means you will have to find a way to protect your plants in high summer. This is usually pretty easy, but few people do it. You can throw a white sheet up on the roof and pull it carefully to where it will do the most good by diffusing the light. You can use old bamboo blinds, or even an orange tarp if that's what you have on hand. The next thing you'll need to do is arrange more airflow. This could include leaving the door open all day, cutting away some of the plastic near the peak of the roof or, if you have the know-how, installing an opening panel at the highest point of the roof. You'll know when you have to institute these measures — you'll walk into the greenhouse one day and almost faint from heat. If you're too hot, so are your plants, so create some ventilation.

More bad stuff: if bad bugs do get inside your greenhouse and you aren't paying attention they could do a lot of damage. This is because they can't just drift away to something more appealing even if they want to (still haven't seen the blueprints and can't find the door) and are now forced to eat what's in front of them, and because you may accidentally be keeping your good bugs outside where they can't help. This is another reason to create a greenhouse that can be open in the summer. The plants are then past most types of damage, they can take the temperature, and there is free passage of good bugs and pollinators into your greenhouse. Oh, that's right! Plants that need insects for pollination will require these critters to have easy access. Leave those doors open, and put in some flowering plants of different colours near the door to catch the eye of wandering bugs.

It never rains in a greenhouse, so when you take holidays from your garden and are revelling in that pattering of rain on your roof, don't forget that the greenhouse plants still need you.

## DESIGN ISSUES I HAVE KNOWN

If you're putting together your own greenhouse or lean-to, here are some thoughts to keep in mind:

- Make the door a decent width. I tried a very tiny door so that I could have more shelving along the sides, but I spent lots of time with grazed knuckles after struggling to get large pots in and out and I dumped the odd seedling tray when it hit the edge of the door. I also couldn't fit handy little tables in there. I swore quite a bit
- Don't waste materials on height, unless you are really tall or can use the top few feet for hanging baskets. If there aren't plants in it, it's wasted space
- Never forget when deciding where plants will go that the top few feet are the hottest
- Make sure you can build in lots of shelving. I've seen beautiful looking greenhouses that weren't planned for shelving and didn't have much space to put anything! Plan as much shelf area as you can. Don't forget that there will be microclimates, with hot/bright at the south and top, receding to cooler/shadier as you work your way down and back. But even your shelves will create shade and you can put your more tender seedlings and shade-tolerant plants in these places
- Plan one stretch of tabletop just for yourself, to dump out and repot a plant, or to spread out your seeds and seed trays
- It's handy to keep two five-gallon buckets under your work table, one to hold soil and one to hold garbage. All those broken plant pots, unreadable tags and plastic bags have to go somewhere

- Hang one large empty hanging basket at eye level if space is short. You can store your clippers, tags and dibbles in it. But first you have to figure out what a dibble is
- I have one galvanized washbasin on the ground in my greenhouse and I wouldn't do without it. I keep it three-quarters full of water, and use it when I need to plunge something sad in for a quick drink or drop some cuttings where they won't dry out. I'm sure it also boosts the humidity, which is good for the plants. You could use a couple of old buckets for this — just swing the hose past them when you're watering, to keep them topped up (or arrange them under the leak in the roof as I do)

## WHAT SHOULD GO IN THE GREENHOUSE?

Seeds and plants that usually struggle to get going because the springs are too late and cold, such as tomatoes and eggplants, love to be in the greenhouse. Squash like it, too. Look at your planting chart to decide what you should start inside in early spring and give them a head start with protection. Of course, it's cold at night still, so either bring your flats back into the house at night, or supply some plugged-in heat in the greenhouse for the first while.

Tropicals that thrive in heat and humidity like to be in there, too. Be careful when you move any tropical from the shade and near-constant temperatures of your house to the exposed windows and cold nights of a spring greenhouse! If in doubt, wait for warm weather, and move your tropicals slowly from the most shaded area, usually the lower northern side, toward the windows, watching for burning as you go. When you reach a safe site, leave them where they are to adapt to the changing seasons, as summer fades and the cool weather of autumn sets in. Many tropicals will burn to a crisp, even in North America, if they get hit with sunlight through glass! You'll also suddenly have to water your houseplants more often as they grow and perspire all day, so be ready for that.

# HOW I USE MY GREENHOUSE

- In early spring, I use it for scattering lettuce seed and I put out cold-weather seeds like miner's lettuce and shrubs
- The greenhouse is a great holding pen for kale and Chinese greens that I want to protect from the bugs until I clean up my garden area
- Potted plants that I stored there for the winter will break dormancy faster, so when I put them outside they've had a head start. These consist of a lot of my porch flowers and herb pots
- I take some of my houseplants out when it gets warmer, because those six months of good growing conditions almost make up for the crummy situation in the house
- In later spring I put my tomato and squash seedlings out to the greenhouse because the added light keeps them from getting leggy. It may still be cool for them at night, though
- When my cuttings have taken in the spring, I pot them up but keep them in the greenhouse so they have good, safe growing conditions

## Houseplant notes

Houseplants will really thrive in a carefully shaded and well-watered greenhouse. If they are given generous amounts of diluted manure tea and moved into a larger pot midsummer, they will put on terrific growth. But they become addicted to that jungle atmosphere, so you will have to take that into account when you take them back inside in the fall. The first impulse is to leave them out there as long as possible to soak up any remaining benefits the greenhouse can give them, but by then you've got the furnace or wood stove fired up and they are coming into a hot, dry atmosphere with wild temperature swings. It's actually better to move them inside earlier, when the house still has its doors and windows open during the day (mid- to late September might be good), so that they can acclimatize as you slowly adapt to your winter conditions.

and I can keep my eye on them for the first few months

♪ In late summer I move potted items like tomatoes and cantaloupe back into the greenhouse to benefit from the shorter period of coolness at night

## WHAT IS THE RIGHT TEMPERATURE?

There are two reasons not to worry about the "right" temperature at which to keep a greenhouse. The first is that most likely you'll have all sorts of plants in there — a begonia in the shade of the planting table, a passionflower vine hanging down near your head. Maybe you'll have some cactuses because you saw them in a Mexican movie and it was hot there; maybe the gardenia your aunt gave you. All of these plants would prefer a different range of heat, and they all look fine, so relax. Second, it's time to realize that even if you've hooked up a heater and improved the ventilation system so that you *can* control the heat, you'll have pockets of heat and cold and will have to adjust the plants accordingly. Plants will withstand an amazingly wide range of temperatures and conditions without your even knowing it. Your best guide is to watch their health and move them around as you see fit. Use your senses and intuition to tell if a plant is happy where it is. A happy plant has a strong colour, good leaf texture, and just plain looks robust. Strangely, you will have achieved the right temperature for the most plants when you yourself feel very comfortable and almost in a holiday mood in your greenhouse!

## SOME SUBTLE SIGNS OF UNWELLNESS

A plant that turns white and papery almost immediately after being put in the greenhouse could have sunburn. We *think* the idea of a greenhouse is to have lots of sun, but the sun has been captured

### Winter in the greenhouse
The greenhouse is a great place into which to drag all your terra cotta pots for the winter, so that they won't split in the frost. You can store your window boxes and hanging baskets in there, too, if they contain perennials. You might also want to sprinkle some lettuce seeds into a planting box and see what you can get.

in a tiny space. I can't remind you often enough to use your own nerve endings to figure out if it's too hot. If you think it is, find something to do about it.

That light blasting through the walls all day can be a killer. If there is no convenient way to shade the space right inside the glass or plastic, tape newsprint, or an other semi-opaque paper to it. If the plant is getting leggy and stretched out, it needs more light. Don't thrust it right into the best light; move it slowly over a few days and stop when you see it start to wilt! Limp leaves mean that either the heat is too strong or the plant hasn't received enough water. Sometimes even after a good watering our plants look floppy. This could be because we've watered only the top half inch of the soil and the rest of the water has trickled out through the bottom. Turn a plant over and out of its pot onto your planting table now and then to see how wet the soil is after a watering. You will be shocked. You will be appalled. You will go back out for your hose.

Sometimes I count to five while watering each plant as a way of convincing myself I'm doing a good job. Another technique is to keep

## "Ask Astilbe"

**Q:** All my greenhouse books suggest emptying and then sterilizing my greenhouse with a bleach mix each spring to prevent disease. How thorough do I have to be?

**A:** Gosh! I bet your underwear is lined up alphabetically by pattern and fabric! Unless you're doing brain surgery in your greenhouse — and honestly, I think there's a better place for that (and leave Bill alone!) — there really isn't anything in that greenhouse so bad that it needs bleaching. I suggest a good cleanout each spring to find slug hideouts, repair holes and retrieve all your old coffee cups, but that should do it. Mildew can be a problem, but venting (leaving doors/windows open) will cure it, as will moving plants around or moving them farther apart. I once heard the owner of a commercial greenhouse lamenting that she had to spray yet again for mildew. I'd seen the same problem at home, and moving the plants in question to an airier location had fixed that. As for insect infestations, the open windows will assist with that as spiders and other predators move in to do their duty. So as much as it gives you the heebie-jeebies, please leave the spiderwebs out of your cleaning regime. And the bleach, too.

an empty water glass in the greenhouse, amongst your plants, and watch how much water is actually going into it during your normal watering. You'll slow down a bit and water longer after that. If your plants still aren't getting enough water, it's time to rethink your heat and lighting.

### Season extenders (other than a greenhouse )

We can't all have a greenhouse in the yard, so here are some more methods for extending your gardening season!

- Choose seeds that are cold-tolerant. Lots of veggies with names, such as Autumn King carrots, Winterkeeper beets or Winter Density lettuce, can be planted earlier (or later) in the season
- Plant in the fall everything you can, such as potatoes, garlic and shallots. They will come up earlier in the spring when you're busy with other things, anyway
- Plant perennials in your garden so that you can gather for longer and with lower cost (Welsh onions, sorrel)
- Use clear plastic draped over sticks or laid right on the ground to create an area that will hold heat longer
- Learn to plant winter vegetables (broccoli, Brussels sprouts, cauliflower, kale) in summer and give them a good start during that long, warm fall
- Keep tending and mulching your overwintering plants so that they can provide for you longer into the fall without suffering stress
- Learn your edible weeds, such as chickweed and miner's lettuce, because they tend to be more adapted to your region's weather and last longer into the winter

# GROWING IN THE DARK

12

For some reason, many of my older gardening books declare that just about everything I want to grow requires "full sun." That's why it's such a puzzle to see perfectly happy specimens growing in the shade or semi-shade. I think those earlier garden writers were making assumptions that just because something is green it needs full light — completely ignoring the healthy forest that might have been growing at their elbow. As we turn back to figuring out how our ancestors did it we start to see more titles on the bookshelves that have to do with taking advantage of plants that grow in the shade, as in forest gardening. Part of our reconsideration is based on our need to pre-serve more trees and wild space on each and every "property," but shade-growing has a few more things going for it. For instance, you don't have to stand over a plant and hold a hose all day if it's growing in shade — it isn't getting the life sucked out of it by the blazing sun. And if you learn to eat a few more of the things that grow in the shade, such as wild greens and low-light berries, you'll have extended your garden area considerably.

Is there really enough food to be drawn from the shade? Case in point: a modern 130-pound human (omnivore) would starve to death on a mountainside if he or she didn't have a full-sun veggie garden (and would have bad hair to boot), but a 300-pound bear (omnivore) would recog-nize that it was surrounded by food in all that shade, would eat what was available and would still look pretty good after a few weeks (its hair would look better, too). We just have to shift our thinking, do some experimenting, and maybe try out some roots and shoots from the nature book along the way. You sneer at this thought? Ever heard of a bear with hemorrhoids?

## WHY ARE WE LEARNING SHADE-GROWING AGAIN?

Sometimes we rent or buy a property that has a lot of shade and there is nothing we can do about it. Even if we could do something about it (like cutting down all the trees), we know that is why the planet is getting sick and that someone has to stop doing it. It could be you. Oh, wait … it *is* you! Or maybe you're in the shade of another building and there is just nothing you can do about that.

Look at that forest model again on page 25. A lot is going on there! You may even see some plants you like, such as ferns and tiny shooting stars growing out of the moss. You'll see things such as huckleberries and salal, which when we do preserve we tend to put in the West Coast

**Microclimate**

Don't forget to "microclimate" your shade. There are different degrees of it, and there is the damp shade under the alders, and the dry shade under the cedars. If the spot gets more than five or six hours of sun a day, plant your "normal" plants and save the shadier spots for the items you'll find in this chapter. Don't forget about light reflection, and how a pale mulch such as pine chips or hay will throw a lot of light back up. So don't regret your shade — fill it with multi-use delights, instead!

"forest clump" out in the middle of our lawns as a nod towards appreciating our wild landscape. It would do much better in its natural shady habitat.

## Things that grow in the forest

Without killing another tree to describe them all (even though it would give me more light), I will note that the woods are full of edible plants. We'd be as healthy as bears if we had to actively seek out feed from our own surroundings (which I admit would be quite time-consuming in this day and age, when we spend more time in coffee shop lineups). In the days before European settlement, there was plenty of food for human consumption and lots left for the bears — salmonberries, salal berries, starflowers, licorice root, wild alliums. Go to your library and look for a book on native foods; note which plants grow in the shade and along forest edges and learn to identify some of them.

### How to get things from the woods

First of all, consider not getting things from the woods. If you have a friend with a wild area, you could take small plants from there, instead. You could keep your eye on new houses going up at the edge of town and be the Plant Early Response Team and save everything you can.

### Three great tips for foraging wild foods

- Don't forget that any food growing on a roadway will be coated with exhaust from passing cars. These residues can be measured in a lab, and the measurable rates drop the farther from the road you get. For best health, harvest as far from a roadway as possible
- Forage with an experienced person the first few times out. Luckily, most of the common foods are easy to recognize and difficult to confuse with anything else, but look at the leaves, stems and growing habits of each plant you pick from to make it easier to identify next time
- Remember that humans already have grocery stores and gardens and have no need to decimate wild foods. Unless you are picking something overwhelmingly prolific, such as blackberries, remember that little critters have only this food to eat and it is not fair to hike in and pick an area clean. Don't pick in quantity at all if you have alternatives, including your own garden at home

If you do go into the woods, pick small plants because they will move better. Take a very good trowel so that you can get all the roots and not just snap off plants that will be left to die. If you find a single plant that you want, keep walking until you find a clump of them. Take a couple of young ones from the clump, and replace the soil and moss as best you can. Put your findings in a plastic bag, with the roots wrapped in moss so you don't lose it on the way home. Plant carefully, in a similar environment, with lots of water, and mulch well with moss. Unless you see hundreds of them, never take a plant for granted as "common." Give all plants huge respect and don't risk the life of one if you don't think you can nurse it through a transplant.

## Ornamentals

If you really don't want your yard to look like just another patch of forest, don't forget all the great ornamentals that tolerate or even prefer partial to full shade. Here's a list of just a few:

- **Ferns** – big and small, feathery and leathery
- **Hostas** – in all their variegated variety
- **Azaleas** – in all their hues
- **Aucuba** – very exotic looking!
- **Crimp leaf and variegated ivies** – can grow up fences or spill out of pots
- **Italian arum** – it has big tropical leaves in the spring and fall and dies down in the summer
- **Periwinkle** – a pretty ground cover that will flower early
- **Pulmonaria** (lungwort, such a yummy name) – it will grow bigger so you can split it up, and it flowers in white, pink and blue
- **Lily of the valley** – can tolerate dry spaces between cedar roots
- **Woodruff and forget-me-nots** – planted together in fairly dense shade, these give a great blue-and-white show in the spring
- **Astilbe** – really easy to grow and gives a flowering plume
- **Lady's mantle** – takes an amazing amount of shade
- **Primrose** – brightens your spring garden
- **Black bamboo** – I've read that it should be in full sun, but mine is growing vigorously in about three hours of sun a day
- **Climbing hydrangea** – can create multi-levels of foliage

Many of the above are considered medicinal, as well, so when the Big Crash comes you'll have some insurance planted in the garden.

One huge benefit of replanting an area with native varieties is that you'll encourage the butterflies and bees that used to hang out in your little backwater to return and perhaps breed in your garden. Some of these butterflies and even birds are becoming rare because they can't find a string of familiar vegetation along their regular migration routes from which to eat or in which to breed, so consider yourself a great helper as you replace some natural life, right down to "weeds" like the funny-looking milkweed.

## Plants, both pretty and useful, that do just fine in six hours of sunlight, thank you very much

Most of the salad plants — such as lettuce, corn salad, sorrel, miner's lettuce (both Siberian and otherwise), Good King Henry, chard, kale — are naturals for a shady spot. Many of the "moist" herbs are happier in part shade than in deep sunlight. Lovage, cicely, angelica, woodruff, chives, wild ginger and all the mint family, including lemon balm and catnip, can create even more uses for your shady area and will attract pollinating insects, too.

Berries will accept a lot more shade than you'd imagine, down to four or five hours of sunlight, although I find my fall-bearing raspberry would like more late-afternoon sun. My strawberries, currants, gooseberries and blueberries and all my brambles seem to produce quite nicely in very few hours of sunlight. I do keep the paths mulched, though, to reflect light.

Peas and potatoes will produce in fewer than six hours of light a day, the potatoes in as little as four, and I even get a decent haul of beans, if there is enough heat in late summer in my area. I have even coaxed a few zucchinis to grow, although my other squash has a chosen spot in the corner where slightly more than six hours of light a day helps it to produce at least a small harvest. So take heart if you are gardening in deep shade. Next time you have someone in your garden, as I have had, with their hands on their hips and looking up with a squint at the circling trees as they tell you you'll have to take them all down, tell them to please stop standing on your harvest when they talk like that!

Once you've tried these traditional garden plants, learn how to forage from the natural foods that are growing right in your yard. Learn to identify huckleberry, thimbleberry, salmonberry and blackberry, experiment with Oregon grape and salal, purslane, miner's lettuce, sheep and wood sorrel, chickweed, thistle roots and wild strawberries. And that's just the tip of the wild-food iceberg.

## Other options for those still faint of heart

Even with all these choices — and the above is just the crack in the door of gloomy delights — some gardeners will still be staring at those trees with dreams of chainsaws whirring in their heads. Light! They need more light.

How about these options: trim away well-chosen branches to let shafts of light through to important parts of the garden. Branches also can be removed in a spiral shape, working around the tree like a circular staircase, so that as the sun passes behind it there are windows of light along the way.

A well-informed tree guy or gal can give you good advice on which branches they can remove without throwing the tree off balance or making it put out crazy growth in inappropriate places. Get lots of quotes — tree people charge a huge range of prices where I live. Our local favourite is the least expensive to hire, which is nice, but also difficult to get your hands on for the same reason. My tree guy actually talked me out of spiralling and thinning because, he said, where I live in coastal British Columbia the tree would just eagerly re-grow those limbs with all its saved energy. I should have had him do just one, so I could see for myself.

# SEEDING AND BREEDING

## 13

The reason Earth was almost completely covered in plants for the first 99 percent of its life is because that was a good way to be! Lots of oxygen, lots of humidity and rain and food for all. It was easy to stay covered in plants, because plants are naturally encoded to propagate in as many ways as they can think up. They could make children from seeds, or if pieces of their branches were broken off by passing animals the plants could also reproduce from the broken sections. Today they will still push children up from their root tips, and if a shrub is in a landslide and mostly covered in soil it will merely grow rootlets

along the buried portions and put out new growth from there. Sometimes a single leaf is all it takes to produce a new plant. And sometimes avid mothers just pop off little miniatures of themselves at a slight distance, or divide themselves into several plants and start off as a clump the next year. Let's look into all of these methods of plant propagation and see how we can turn our yards into thriving masses of greenery merely by using the plant's own need to reproduce! Ain't procreation fun?

## Making children from seed

This is the most obvious way of creating plants and one of the easiest to try. We've already looked at growing plants from seeds, but here are a few further details to make life easier, or at least more understandable.

Most of the seeds a beginner buys will be for annual flowers or vegetables and these are pretty straightforward. Make them wet, give them light, then give them food. When people begin to gather their own seeds for perennial flowers and shrubs and trees, they start to run into trouble. For one thing, a lot of the plants that grow in temperate North America evolved in step with our seasons. In the fall, the seeds would drop to the ground, in winter they'd have a spell of cold, and in spring when things warmed up enough to signal the seeds they it would begin to grow. Obviously they learned the hard way that if they sprouted when they hit the ground and felt those moist autumnal rains they would have their tender little greens frozen off! There are exceptions to this, but if you've tried to grow certain bushes or lilies without any luck you will have to try again, using "fake winter." You can fake winter by putting the seeds in the fridge, either dry or packed in dampish sand. It could take two to three months of this, but you can leave them longer if necessary. Then take them out and plant them in pots, and keep them damp and in some shade till you see some action.

You also could try some "real" winter. Plant the seeds in the late fall and put the pots in a cold greenhouse or under the steps. Pull it out in spring and let some filtered sun hit it slowly and gently. Some plants take two full years of this to germinate, so you can imagine what kinds of gardening fanatics are out there! Myself not included, of course.

### Cross-breeding

One thing new gardeners don't always recognize is the great excitement plants find in breeding with each other. Plant two types of squash beside each other, or two hues of columbine, and look out! Those plants will have created a new gene structure before you can blink an eye. The results may or may not be pleasing. Although I've heard that most nut tree crosses create quite edible results, it is well known that squash, when they cross, are likely to produce a pretty but tasteless progeny.

Tomatoes should be kept 10 feet apart if you want to save seed, lettuce and bush beans 20 feet apart, and the range just goes up from there. Many plants such as the whole cole family (Brussels sprouts, cabbage, broccoli), cucumbers, eggplants, the mustards, peppers and the squash family need a half mile between them to keep those pesky pollinators from stirring those genes.

These distances still make sense to country folks, who have miles between them, but the city dweller will have to snoop through many backyards to see if it is safe to take seeds that may no longer be what they seem. Don't fret, though — this is a perfect reason to support all the small organic-seed businesses that are sprouting up, to protect our endangered open pollinated seeds.

## Pieces of broken branches

It sounds too easy, but try this. Using sharp pruners, take some cuttings, from the end of local currant bushes, hardy hibiscus, grapes, forsythia and anything else that will hold still for you. Visit friends and ask them if you can clip your way through their yard. Don't forget to label each batch of cuttings as you go. Take cuttings between late October and early March for effort-free rooting; they will actually take at any time of year with some fuss, but who needs fuss?

**Pure as a sunflower**

Technically, different varieties of sunflower need two to five miles between them to ensure "pure" uncrossed seed, much to the amazement of our own local sunflower grower, who was selling seed packets from the many varieties grown in her yard.

Take home your labelled bundles of foot-long pieces of branch and bury them to half their length, cut-end down, in a loose soil mix. Put them under the stairs or in a cold greenhouse, or against the north side of the house. Make sure they're damp. The secret, anthropomorphically speaking, is that these cuttings will wake up all groggy in the spring, do some yawns and stretches, suddenly say "Holy smoke! No roots!" and promptly grow some. You can shake out the pot gently in early summer and you'll see roots on many of the cuttings. If the cuttings have withered, toss them in the compost heap; then pot up the others before the new roots get dry in the sun. Keep these plants moist until their roots have truly got going.

A fully leafed-out plant that is busy sucking water from its very important roots will get a bit snotty with you for cutting it off, so if you take cuttings in the summer try these techniques: take your cutting early in the day or when the plant has been well-watered, and drop it immediately into a pail of water. Pinch back the leaves to the very last bit near the tip so it will have less to support, and if it has big stiff leaves cut these down by half, so that they can still do their work but without as much strain.

Push the cutting into your loose rooting medium. The more humid you keep it the better, because you have just amputated its water supply and now have to replace all the work it did.

Nurseries will tell you that your luck will improve if you buy rooting hormone, but it will improve even more if you recall that rooting hormone comes from trees. If you can plan to get some willow cuttings at the same time as your plant cuttings, you can mash and twist these and let them sit in a bucket, then let your cuttings sit in this water for a couple of days before planting in a loose soil mix. I know that willows don't come labelled "hardwood" and "softwood" as the hormone in the stores does, but this makes life easier, yes?

### The medium is the mess

Clay is a bad rooting medium because it's too dense and doesn't have enough room for that important oxygen we know plants need.

# Children from root tips

Sometimes you'll notice a little plum tree coming out of the ground several feet from an adult tree. This is growing from the parent plant's roots, and can be cut off and carried away. Some trees put out many of these babies, and it makes us feel greedy to take them all, but make sure you actually like the taste of the fruit before you start hundreds of its children. If you do want that little tree, take a good, sharp shovel and some sturdy clippers and, if it's a dry day, make sure you have a bucket of water to drop the little pup into so you can get it home without dehydrating it. Now draw an imaginary line from the big tree to the small one so you'll know where the root connects them, and start easing up that little tyke. It will resist where it is connected to the big tree, but once you've found that root cut it off cleanly, leaving as much new root on the baby as possible. It may also carry on again from there and you will have to cut the continuing root off on the other side, as well, to free it.

If you get down there and realize that the pup has not developed any true roots from its base, it will be hard to grow; just cover over that section and look for another one. Some trees put up many suckers at the base that are all good potential tree-lets, but may have the same problem: if they have no true roots of their own, you will have to mollycoddle them until they grow some. But give it a try, since you should remove all these suckers anyway, and trying is free!

When you are digging away in a garden, at times you will accidentally cut into shrub roots and notice what looks like a tiny growing bump, or even just a fresh, shiny patch on the top of the root or at the tip of it. It's worth taking this piece home and putting it in some loose soil to see if it receives the same wake-up call as the others ("Oh my god! Where's my body? Better grow a new one out of this bud!")

**Don't be too afraid of failure**

Take your cuttings gently from spots where you think pruning is required anyway. Check chapter 8 and make your cut according to the pruning diagram, so that a tidy new branch will come out facing the right way. But don't sweat about it. Catch gardening friends early and ask them to save the cuttings for you when they prune, rather than toss them on the compost heap. This will take off some of the pressure!

## Growing roots along their buried portions

Sometimes you'll see a lazy azalea or droopy honeysuckle that has started a new root along the stem where it has touched the soil. It might give you the idea that this could be done on purpose, and you would be right. Many shrubs and vines can be encouraged to touch the soil and may put out a root at that spot. You can help with that decision by making sure there is a node present where the stem hits the soil (although some plants will just create one). Use some bent wire to keep the branch from springing back up, and pile some soil on top of the newly grounded stem to keep the area moist and make the stem think this is a good area from which to root.

One day, you'll see little growing leaves coming out of the top of the soil and you can gently uproot the whole branch. Cut the branch off about one inch behind the new roots, then transplant your new baby. This is the method I use for breeding more boysenberry bushes. I just keep forcing a branch down and piling it with soil until I see that new bud!

## A single leaf or branch tip

You've seen this method used with African violets and it does seem to be more useful for the tropical plants in general, so try it out on your houseplants. Piggyback plants and the African violet are the best known for single-leaf propagation, but try a branch tip, with a piece of stem, if you have a begonia, coleus, hoya, arrowhead or dieffenbachia. Bury lots of stem in the medium, and see if you can keep it moist and warm enough that it will manage to put out a root for you.

## Popping off little miniatures

This is the easiest way of propagating plants. You merely reach down, pop a baby off and say "thank you very much!" Potatoes are the first example of this that comes to mind, and the banana potato has even gone to the extent of growing little potatoes, with a tiny leaf already

attached, along its above-ground stem. Saves digging, you know. You'll often see little bulbs forming on the stem of your lilies, too, and these can
be picked off and planted. Strawberries are another propagation winner. After only a year or two,
those babies will be climbing over the planter box
edges and running down the path. Just pick them
off the stem and replant them wherever you want.

## Plants that divide themselves

The most obvious of these are plants like lilies,
garlic and shallots. When you dig one up, you see
that the root is actually in segments that can be
pulled apart and replanted. As a rule of thumb,
the smaller and less developed the segment, the
longer it will take to flower, which could mean a
few years for the lily.

Other plants with thick, fibrous roots aren't
quite as easy to divide. You'll see a clump of
hostas, or daisies or phlox in the spring, with a
number of shoots coming up several inches apart
from what looks like the same root. To divide
plants like these, you need tools! An old bread
knife, a good shovel, pruners, or two small gardening forks might do the trick. To divide the
clump, dig around the edges and pull some soil
away from at least one side of the root, then dig
a tiny way underneath and lift with your shovel to
loosen the plant. Now hunker down and take a
look at how those shoots are attached. Maybe you
can cut out a few plantlets with pruners. Perhaps
you can pry some off by gently teasing with your
hands, which is a preferable method.

But some roots, like those of the hosta, are
actually like a loaf of very dense bread and you
can cut out thick slices and plant them individually without any apparent damage to the mom.
Bamboo is hard to separate but even small bits, if
you've made sure there is root coming out from
under a piece of the rhizome, will take if you give
them lots of time. Iris, rhubarb and red-hot poker
are hard to tear up and you may need a small
machete to break apart the root clumps, but you'll
be amazed at how little that bothers them. If
there's lots of dirt and muck, spray it with a jet of

water from your hose so you can have a clear viewing area. The act of ripping up these plants might feel savage, but the plant's goal is to reproduce and you're helping it do just that. Sometimes it's worth getting an experienced gardener to separate some plants for you, so you can see how it's done and how quickly the plants recover from major surgery. Actually, it damages the plant less to be pulled apart properly than to have you timidly pull off young shoots by trial and error because you haven't got a proper view of the root mass. This happens with raspberries a lot — we pull on the babies growing around the edges, and only succeed in snapping them off and killing them.

Just keep in mind that you should cut rather than tear the roots unless you can tear them with minimal tissue injury, and that you should replant the original plant quickly and hose it down to reduce trauma. Also remember that all those little

## "Ask Astilbe"

**Q:** Okay, Astilbe, dividing plants sounds too easy. What are the most likely things I'll do wrong?

**A:** First, you'll get greedy. You'll say, "Why should I take a puny little piece off the end when I can try and root the whole branch?" Maybe it has something to do with how far from the tip a cutting wants to send certain hormones, but there seems to be a point of diminishing returns at which the more you take, the less likely the piece is to grow roots. But you'll want at least a few nodes on your cutting, some to put out leaves near the top, and some along the stem under the soil, in case it wants to root from there. The second likely mistake is to plant the cutting so shallowly that it's not in contact with lots of moist soil. Sticking it in a couple of inches won't do it. Half its length is more like it, and I've seen some situations in which the cutting was completely buried! The third problem is burning the cuttings, especially in the summer. They want to be warm, but without roots they can't keep those leaves wet enough to take strong light. So be considerate and give them shade or indirect light if you can't keep the soil moist. The last common problem is giving up on them too soon. Some cuttings take a long time to develop, and if you stuck them in the shade outside you might be surprised to see them putting out shoots long after you've given them up for dead. See? Not so bad. If you really want something to worry about, go into weather-reporting! Or stocks! Or world politics! Or …

babies have to be kept moist with a layer of soil or moss until you can get them into dirt again.

The best time to divide a plant is in the spring, since there is no foliage to shred accidentally and you can better see what you're doing. If you do have to work in the summer, remove any damaged leaves and cut back any others so that the new plant can concentrate on growing roots and not have to pump water into so many eager leaves. Fall and winter are also fine times to divide plants.

# EAT IT NOW
# (OR STORE IT FOR LATER)

## 14

## EASY MEALS FOR
## THE NOT-SO-FAINT-HEARTED COOK

People on the run aren't used to having to cook with the miscellaneous and strangely timed produce that will come out of their first garden. The amount of that harvest may be too small to give a share to each of the family, and won't wait in the fridge while the rest catches up. Here are three one-pot, multi-veggie dishes that will take any combination of fresh garden harvest along with whatever you have in the fridge. Recipes are offered as suggestions, since people have very different ideas of what they like in their food, how small it should be cut up and what they absolutely don't want to eat. Look at the following three — Hey! I can only count to three! — as frames on which to hang a multitude of experiments.

## Fried rice

Whatever you do in your life, learn to cook rice. Have some with your current dinner and stick the rest in the fridge for the next day — it fries better when it's cold. Pour some cooking oil into a big frying pan or wok and set the burner at medium high. Chop a small onion (or a big one, or a medium one) and one, two or three stalks of celery into the pan. While that is cooking, add at least a couple of spoonfuls of any of the following: soy sauce, teriyaki sauce, hoisin, black bean sauce, Chinese barbecue sauce, or a crushed chicken bouillon cube in hot water. If you vary the combinations each week, you'll quickly get an idea of how each condiment affects the flavour or the dish. Or hey! Leave them out! While this cooks, add small handfuls of garden produce such as under-size carrots, shelled peas, broccoli leaves, stems and florets, bok choy, cauliflower stems or florets, snow pea pods — and a squish of garlic. Let this cook for a few minutes and add a bit more oil or sauce, tasting as you go. Then throw in the cold rice and separate the grains by pounding on it. Chop in some green onions, finely sliced lettuce and, if you eat meat, add fine slices of it now. For an authentic touch, push the mixture to the sides of the pan, pour a little oil in the hole in the centre, and break in an egg. The egg lends its own flavour and texture and it adds protein to a dish that might not otherwise fulfill a vegetarian diet. You can either let the egg cook solid, cut it in strips and blend it with the rice, or merely break the yolk, scramble it and stir it into the mix. Cover the pan and leave it for a minute to make sure the egg is cooked, then serve with sesame oil and sesame seeds.

## Noodle soup

I've heard our local nutritionist complain about the rash of Asian noodle soup mixes on the market. They do lack nutrients, but they certainly make a good base for a great vegetable soup! Pour a quarter cup more than the suggested quantity of water into a saucepan; cut broccoli, carrots, green onions, mushrooms, small beans, slices of kale leaves, etc., into the water. When it reaches a boil, add the noodle mix and follow directions for adding the flavour packet at the end. Break one egg into the pot and stir it (egg swirl soup! Cool!) until the egg is cooked. If you have it, add a few drops of sesame oil to this, too.

## Fried noodles

Start as with fried rice, with any amount of celery and onions. Add your flavouring as for the rice dish, and any amount of zucchini, broccoli, cauliflower, peas, sliced kale or chard. Boil and strain the noodles, or push the vegetables up the sides of the pan and pour in a couple of cups of water. Add a cup (or less, or two cups) of dried noodles and cover. Check to see that there is adequate water in the pan to soften the noodles completely. When they are soft, break in your egg, stir and cover again. Add green onion or cooked meat and heat for a couple of minutes.

There! Three easy ways to use odd amounts of vegetables.

## WHAT SHOULD I DO WITH ALL THE FRESH PRODUCE?

Here are a few miscellaneous recipes for fresh garden produce. These recipes are so easy that even I use them! Heck, some of them are based on much longer recipes from which I threw away the rest of the ingredients.

### Quick potato salad (you'll never guess what's in this!!)

Steam baby potatoes and carrots and other veggies, toss with garlic, oil, salt and pepper, a touch of mayo, and garden herbs such as oregano and dill. As you can see, drizzling just about anything with garlic, oil and just a dab of mayo will satisfy the laziest or most overworked cook among us! Garlic, olive oil, mayo and lemon juice also make a fast, easy salad dressing for your surprise salad.

## Purple cabbage

Cut the cabbage off at the base, just under where it swells into a ball, and peel off the outer, chewed-on leaves. Slice the head of cabbage into two halves, then slice sideways into mouth-size pieces. These can be stored in a plastic bag in the fridge for a couple of days, but will lose nutrients. To use it, put the desired amount into a bowl and pour over it a capful or two of olive oil. Toss with a spoonful or two of mayo and a squirt of lemon juice. Chop some chives or green onions over it and stir. This tastes great with salted sunflower seeds over it. Even people who don't like cabbage will eat this.

## Green cabbage

Do the same as with the purple cabbage until you've got it sliced up. You can treat it the same way, or dump it into a shallow pan with a tablespoon of water, a splash of soy sauce and a small splash of teriyaki sauce. Put the lid on. Turn the burner to medium heat and let it bubble until the cabbage is soft. This is good with faux Asian food. It's an imitation of a Korean dish and it satisfies the need for salt.

## Carrots

Cut off the green top and any chewed-on bits. No need to peel the rest. Chop it into eraser-size pieces, then steam or nuke them for a few minutes until they are soft. Strain them. Put a squish of garlic over them, and the usual drizzle of oil and mayo. Toss everything until covered. This is so delicious that I eat it late at night. It's a much healthier snack than junk food!

## Favourite beans

Slice beans any which way and steam them. Next, toss fresh-picked, store-bought fresh or canned mushrooms, sliced, into a frying pan. Cook them in butter and pepper until they are light brown.

Toss in the steamed beans and stir them around in there, too, until they are just a tiny bit brown.

## Winter squash

First-time gardeners are always amazed to see squashes such as Hubbard and buttercup blowing up like giant warts out of the greenery in their garden. Happily, squash always tastes better than it looks. After curing, you may have to use an axe to it.

Some squashes have quite a thin skin and you can eat this if you wish. Some people save all the seeds, just like pumpkinseeds, and eat them, too! Put the seeds in a bowl of warm water and scrub the stringy bits off with your fingers. Wash, dry on newspapers, then spread the seeds onto an oiled baking sheet. Bake at 250°F (or put the pan on your wood stove) until the seeds turn light brown. Eat plain, or with salt, or try some spices from your cupboard.

Oh, right! We still have the squash left!

Of course, you can hack a squash into manageable pieces and bake it face down on a buttered baking pan at 400°F for about 45 minutes. Then slather it with butter and a touch of maple syrup, or sprinkle some Parmesan cheese onto it and add salt and pepper to taste.

## Fall garden medley (can be called tomato sauce if you freeze the excess!)

Pick any remaining tomatoes before they rot. Drop them into boiling water until the skin cracks, then lift them out and drop into cool water. Pull the skin off. Chop crudely into the shape of your favourite politician's nose, and drop into a heavy pan with a tablespoon of oil.

Clean up after the tomatoes, and pick all your remaining zucchinis. Rinse, cut off any dirty ends and cut into the approximate shape of your favourite politician's right kidney. Oh, wait, that's getting hard. Just cut them up and throw them in. Throw in the equivalent of one big onion and squish in some of your fall garlic. If you grew

### Flying saucers

Cut some ripe tomatoes in half and put them on an oiled baking sheet. Mix herbs like oregano and thyme with Parmesan cheese and bread crumbs, and salt and pepper, and mound this mixture onto the tomatoes. Then put the whole rocky mess under the grill for a few minutes until the crumbs brown.

### Hey! Did I just say Parmesan cheese?

Lots of fresh veggies taste good with Parmesan cheese. If you aren't already converted, start keeping small amounts of freshly shredded (not that stuff in the can) cheese in your fridge. It's especially good on zucchinis and tomatoes.

puny little celery stalks, slice them up and throw them in, too. And any peppers. Don't worry about politician shapes. Add lots of oregano and thyme. And scarlet runner beans. You get the picture. Let this cook for a long time and eat it as soup, or freeze it for pouring over pasta later in the winter.

## Fried green tomatoes

If it looks as though your garden is going to freeze over before the last of the tomatoes are ripe, try this: mix cornmeal, salt and pepper together in a paper bag and then pour the mix onto a big flat plate. Cut your green tomatoes into slices and wipe both sides through this mix. Heat a big frying pan with vegetable oil and when it's hot plop the tomato slices in, a few at a time, and fry them on both sides until light brown.

## Salsa

If you haven't grown tomatillos before, start now! They are related to tomatoes, but are tougher, and won't die of every stupid blight that blows through your yard. And they are an important component of real salsa!

Try this: finely chop into a bowl a couple of cloves of garlic, a small handful of cilantro, a small onion, your current crop of tomatillos and a tiny bit of hot pepper, and add a dash of salt. You'll notice that I'm not worried about amounts, and that's because you will play with the amounts as you get used to the flavours (more cilantro? Ready for more hot pepper?). Besides, there's no sense in saying you need six tomatillos if you have only five ready to pick. Make your recipes fit your garden, instead of the other way around!

## STOP, ALREADY!

You may end up with more haul from your garden than you can eat right away, in which case you get a big gold star. Follow these tips to keep that produce ready to eat when you want it. The

alternative is a big stinking pile of mush, so read carefully!

## Apples

Handle them carefully so that they don't bruise, and lay them carefully in a box or basket in a very cool place such as a basement. Don't store apples near other harvest goodies — they emit a gas that promotes sprouting in many other plants!

## Cabbage

Leave the stem and roots on, but tear off the first couple of layers of leaf to check for tiny slugs. They would have quite the party on your stored cabbage before you discovered their now giant, heaving bodies where your squash used to be. Store your heads of cabbage in a very humid, cool place like an unheated basement or outbuilding. They will keep for a long time.

## Garlic

Leave garlic until the tops dry, then pull them up, knock the soil off them and leave them out to dry further for a few days. After a couple of days go by, gently rub off some more soil and chop off all but an inch of root and top. Bring them in and store them like your onions, in any airy, dry place, with enough warmth to keep the humidity from rotting them. If they start to sprout in early February, take them outside and split them into cloves, replant them, give them a good mulching, and see if you can get new heads out of them next year.

## Onions

When the tops have died down, wait again for a stretch of clear weather, pull the onions up gently and place them on the soil. Roll them over in the sun for a couple of days, then cut off all but an inch of the dried top and put them in that nice dry spot where the potatoes are, under the deck or in a warm room. They can cure like this for a week or so. Then pack them in a shallow box. The books say to put the box in a cool spot, but I find that this is too humid and they start to rot; now I leave them one layer deep in baskets under the couch. They never go bad on me there. Onions will keep for months. If yours are pretty tiny when you dig them up, just cure them as usual and plant them out next spring to try again with a little more manure tea and sunshine.

## Potatoes

If you decide to store potatoes, wait until the tops have died down and the weather looks like it will be clear for the day. Needing a good rain for some other purpose generally causes clear weather, so wait for it. Next, carefully dig up your whole potato patch. Check each potato for any damage from your digger, because those ones won't keep; send them right to the kitchen for washing. Pick out the little golf ball-size ones for replanting. Leave the rest on the soil surface for at least a day, turning them once in a while. Lay them in a dry spot out of the sun (under a deck or in the garage) for about 10 days. This will "cure" them, but I'm still not sure of what. Then pack them in paper bags and put them in the back of a dark cupboard. They'll be dormant for a few months, and will keep easily during this time. If they break dormancy by trying to grow shoots and you catch them early enough, you can move them to a cooler spot to slow them down. Otherwise, keep them dark and wait until March to plant them back out, with the shoots spread in the soil and well-covered with soil and mulch.

## Root crops

Try leaving carrots, potatoes, parsnips and beets in the soil into the winter. Mulch them with your fall weeding or some straw if you have it, and dig them up throughout winter as you need them. Mark the rows with sticks so that you'll remember where they were. If you don't dig them up, they will grow the second year and all but the potatoes will put up a seed head. If this happens, you can plant these seeds the following spring. Neat!

## Squashes (Hubbard, acorn, pumpkins, spaghetti, butternut)

If you tried some nice winter squash, good for you. Leave squashes on the vine as long as you can stand it. Early October is a good time to start curing them. Cut the stem about an inch from the, uh, fruit or vegetable or whatever that is, and leave the things out there in the autumn sun for a couple of weeks, sitting on a handful of hay or twigs to keep them off the ground. If it rains a lot, or looks as if it will freeze hard, bring them in. Handle them gently so that you don't bruise the flesh. Put them in a south window or other bright, warm place and turn them for a couple more weeks, but you can leave them on the windowsill for up to three months. I know this for sure. If the windowsill isn't a good spot, carefully put them up on a dry shelf in the kitchen or hall. Don't let your squashes touch each other, and if you see rot starting eat those ones right away. If you see a bit of mould on the skins you can wipe it with an oily rag (vegetable oil — not that WD-40 stuff), but keep an eye on those ones. Properly cured squash will keep for several months. Yummy!

# GARDEN ACTIVITIES YOU CAN DO FROM A LAWN CHAIR

## 15

Several new questions will occur to you as you watch your garden grow. Although some may seek the answers through the use of expensive testing equipment and multiple visits to the plant doctor, good answers are easily discovered with the use of a simple lawn chair. A comfortable kitchen chair (or even a stump) can be substituted for the lawn chair, but the final choice must be (1) comfortable to sit in for at least 17 minutes and (2) easy to move throughout the garden and into the shade. The chair should be near a small flat surface on which to perch a cool drink, and must be far enough from the house that the call of children and ring of the telephone can be ignored. And sometimes you just have to close the connecting door.

## Other important materials

For the following activities you must first trust that you are actually a lot smarter than you think. Between your intuition and your latent instincts, you possess a lot of ability to answer your own questions once you've put yourself through the paces a few times. The suggestions here will allow you to try out your skills in a safe environment — and remember, you can only get better and better at learning from your garden.

## ACTIVITY #1 — "WHAT THE HECK IS WRONG?"

Here we prove that all answers come to those who sit and mull. We realize we have the answers to the question, "What the heck is wrong with my garden?"

At various times throughout the season, we tend to notice that one or another crop is not exactly matching the picture in the gardening book. Inevitably, ours is slightly less perky, perhaps more rundown, mangy or, well, different. But that's okay, because we all have to start somewhere.

On a day of comfortable temperature, take a refreshing drink out to your garden and sit in your chair. Stare at your garden while repeating your question "What the heck is wrong with my garden?" The interesting fact is, that you know what is wrong, or you will know when you have stared at your garden for several minutes. First of all you will hear the spirit of Bill, the community nag, hovering over your shoulder and whispering, "You should have watered it on Sunday night." You may even choose that moment to get up and turn on the hose. Returning to your seat, you will remind yourself that you were going to mulch those berry bushes, because they just look a little parched, somehow. You will then get up, cross the yard, take the carpet off the hay bale and peel off a couple of good handfuls to spread around the newly watered roots. You will return to your chair. See? You really do know what's wrong. Even if you only make the decision to do things differently next year, you can gain a lot of insight by simply observing your garden while it grows and listening to what it tells you.

If your inner voice says, "That's terrible soil, the plants are just sickly," then starting now you will mulch and feed the soil so that next year the plants have a good start. You may decide to put down planks so that you aren't compacting the soil. Make notes of all these things, to add to your gardening repertoire.

If you have trouble coming up with answers to your gardening problems, pretend that the biggest garden expert in the whole area is standing beside you. This could even be a relative, such as Aunt Matty. You probably know exactly what that genius would say about improving your garden. Just do it! And if all of the above fails you can actually ask Bill, or your Aunt Matty, to come over and tell you what is wrong with your garden. And as your teacher stands beside you in the dying sunlight and goes on and on, in your mind you'll hear yourself saying, "I know, I know! *I knew that!*"

## "Ask Astilbe"

**Q:** What are some sensible steps to figure out what is going wrong if I see an ill-looking plant in my garden?

**A:** Using your air/water/food/light list should just about cover it. For instance, if you find bugs on your sick plant you should remember that bugs are more attracted to the weaker plants, like bullies in a schoolyard. And some plants, like people, just didn't get a good start in life. Although it is illegal to put people on the compost heap, this is where some feeble plants should end up so that they can try again in another life. Some folks leave sick plants in the garden, since they are a magnet for bugs; because the bugs have lots to eat, they tend to leave the rest alone. You can then wait for the predator insects or birds to look after it, or you can carefully carry it to the end of the yard. But if you do think it is a water or food issue, just make the change and watch again.

# ACTIVITY #2 – "WHEN DO I PICK IT?"

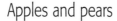

Here we reflect on a crucial issue of timing: "Now that it's growing, how can I tell when it's ripe?" This question is especially pressing for people who have spent 20 years hovering over the produce section of the grocery store, looking at properly ripened vegetables. But that's okay — we've been trained not to fall back on obvious cues. Of course, the six-year-old child next door already has a method for checking ripeness, and it's called the take-a-taste-make-a-face-and-spit test. You can improve on this method, but only slightly. Sensing and tasting are great ways to learn about fruit ripeness. The information will stick in your brain, and if the food actually is unripe you can always spit it out. Now, place your lawn chair in the midst of your slowly ripening garden and observe the fruit of your labours. Here is a kick-start to help you with good timing.

## Apples and pears

You will be delighted to know that all the previous reinforcement concerning honing your observational skills is about to be put to the test. When you're teaching yourself to test tree fruit, don't forget to let texture and scent fill in the gaps for you. Some fruit will develop some "give" when you squeeze it with your whole hand. Some apples are hard to decide on, no matter how hard you look, smell or grip them. My local deer used to come by each morning and pull off a single apple, give it a quick chew and spit it out. I knew the apples were ready when the deer stopped leaving them on the ground. So don't forget to taste your apples (you can sample one that the deer have picked), or cut one open and see if the seeds have ripened to their usual dark brown shiny selves. Pears are hard to judge. Generally softness will give some varieties away, but others are ripe in their crisp stage. Again, tasting is best, and check for that heady aroma, as well.

## Berries

These are prime items for the taste test. Most bramble fruit (blackberries, raspberries, and anything else that looks remotely like them) will be plump and generally have lost that glossy look when they are ripe. If they come loose easily when you pull gently, they're prime to eat. If they don't come off easily, leave them to ripen and try again in a day or two. Sit in your chair and watch a bush for a few minutes. Look at the state of the different berries. I bet you will be able to pick out the bestest of the best if you use your intuition and observational skills! And use the all-important taste test every day or two — it will teach you quickly how to pick good berries. Sweetness is a great criterion.

## Carrots, beets, onions, cabbages

All of these can be eaten as soon as they are big enough to focus your eyes on, but obviously if you eat them when they're very tiny you will have a much smaller harvest of food than if you left them to get to "grocery store" size. Nothing much will happen if you leave your root crops in too long, so once they reach what you consider a decent size you can eat them as you need them.

## Garlic

You can pick your garlic young if you run out of them in the kitchen. They just might seem a bit watery. Don't forget to cut the young flower stems as you see them arise, and eat them in salad or stir-fry. If you fry a chopped-up garlic leaf in oil before you cook, you'll get the garlic flavour without pulling up your garlic bulbs too soon.

## Greens

Garden greens such as lettuce, corn salad and bok choy can have their leaves nibbled as soon as you want them but, obviously, if you let the plant get a head start it will be happier and more robust. Toward the heat of summer, though, many

leaves will get a bitter taste and put up a seed head. By this point some of the seed heads taste better than the leaves, so you can still get some edibles off the plant before it expires from the energy of going to seed.

## Peas, beans

Pea and bean pods have a healthy, full glow when they are ripe, then they become dull-looking quite quickly and lose flavour. It's good to pick your peas and beans just a bit on the early side, so you can get full pleasure from them.

## "Ask Astilbe"

**Q:** My garden got off to a good start, and then I went off on a Vegan Clairvoyants for Peace walking tour, and now my garden is a mess. (I should have known, right?) Can I save it now?

**A:** It's probably quite weedy and dry, right? (Not bad for a greenhorn.) First of all, give it a long, long watering before weeding. If you pull out the weeds first, all that hot sun will hit the turned soil around your dry plants and they'll really suffer. Disturbing all that dry soil by pulling the weeds out when the vegetable roots may be near the surface also will make the veggies very unhappy. So water well, and trim all the weeds down with shears to just below where they want to go to seed. This will keep the soil covered and intact. Pull out any lettuce, bok choy or radish that is going to seed, unless you want to save one for seeds for next year. Cut the tips off tomato and squash plants so they'll have the energy to ripen what fruit they have on them. Pick off any tiny fruit that looks as if it might not make it (use your intuition). If it's late in the season, plants will never have time to produce fruit from the flower stage, so save them the trouble by pinching off the flowers as well and concentrate on what is on the plant. For instance, cut a squash vine to just beyond the last decent-size fruit. Pinch off all flowers and even a few leaves from the tomato plants. If beans and peas haven't been picked and the seeds are starting to dry in the pods, you could try a last-ditch effort by picking every single one and seeing if the plant will squeeze out a few final flowers before fall. Or you could let them continue to dry on the plant and harvest them in the fall as, ta-dah, dried beans and peas for soup, or for replanting next year. Otherwise, cut off all way-past-it plants at the soil surface (the roots will add nitrogen to the soil) and compost the debris for next year. You could also use your chopped ends (minus weeds' seed tops) to lay along the roots of living plants to keep the soil cool and evenly moist.

## Potatoes

Pick potatoes any time! They're wonderful steamed with young dill when they're very tiny. Of course, you lose out on size since they plump out more at the end of the growing season. The glory of having lots of potatoes is in pulling up a plant every week or so through the summer. Then you end up with the big honkers to save for winter!

## Squashes

Zucchinis are edible when tiny, but obviously you'll get more bang for your buck if you give them another couple of days to put on some size. Use your new observational skills to decide at what point the healthy shine starts to flatten out, because you'd be right in deciding to eat it before that point. Unlike winter squash, zucchinis really lose flavour when they hit Zeppelin size. I might suggest that picking zukes when they are as long as your foot is a good rule of thumb, unless you're a basketball player. Other squashes, like butternut and pumpkin, are best left on the vine as long as you can stand it — right into fall if possible. But you can eat them at an inch long, if you want.

## ACTIVITY #3 — "WHAT NEEDS TO CHANGE?"

Here, you lounge in your chair, rub your chin and wonder "What will I do differently next year?"

Gardening is like the rest of the life process — we learn a little more each year (I'm getting a new chair, for one thing) and, when we achieve true wisdom, it means we are actually using our acquired knowledge. Look at your growing area as a completely dynamic work area. Garden beds can become bigger or smaller. This year's potato patch can be next year's carrot bed. Containers can come and go, new crops can be tried, trellises can rise and fall with the need for scarlet runner beans. If you're busy one year, plant the whole thing in potatoes, water it twice in the dry season and otherwise leave the whole thing on its own. It'll all be there next year, waiting to go. Different hues of flowers can be moved around the yard to complement new shrubs and fences.

Garden journals are a good idea about now. You can jot down findings while they're still fresh in your mind, so you won't be standing there next year rubbing your head and saying, "I had a brilliant idea for this corner, now what was it?" Any old school scribbler will make a fine journal and "any time" is a good time to start, even if it's just notes on what you would do better, or sooner or, especially, more. Since you're standing there with a scribbler in your hand, this is also an excellent time to draw a quick map of the yard and where everything ended up, in case you want to rotate your "crops" next year. Most gardening books suggest doing this in the spring, but old flea-bitten gardeners like me know that you'll be changing your mind, tucking in the odd tray of plantlets, looking for a place for those last 50 pea seeds and otherwise making loose with your original garden map. So the end of the season is the best place to map, note and wish.

Since a journal has to please only you, use it to your own maximum advantage. Put the book in a plastic bag under your seed box and get in the habit of using it for notes — because if you don't remember what to do differently next year, that old grouch Bill will be sure to remind you.

## The overview

Here are some notes you might want to make in your journal (right after mentioning what year it is, and sketching the map):

- What you planted
- How it did
- What did terribly and what did well
- What you will never do again
- Some hints and ideas for next year
- And so on

# AFTERWORD

## Read Me When You're Down

Into every gardener's life a little rain must fall. Okay, it was a torrent, and it washed away your petunias. And slugs ate all of your bean plants to stumps, and the dog trampled your tomatoes. An early freeze got in the way of your Eggplant Empire and the carrots failed to come up. You know that, secretly, Bill accuses you of being a bad gardener, and your Aunt Matty taunts you on her weekly visits. "Ha!" she says, "You call that a garden? Go shopping! *Buy* a carrot!" (wicked laughter).

Do you know what an experienced gardener would do with these disasters — after the 17th time the freeze stymied the eggplant and the ninth time the dog trampled the tomatoes? Besides sending auntie on a trip to Spuzzum for ice cream so they wouldn't have to hear her taunting cry? An experienced gardener would just figure out what to do next year and would plant again. And again. It's all right. No problem. This is about process, and about being outside and hearing the bees buzz. Crops have been getting trampled for centuries. We've just got to look after them differently next year, that's all.

To the goal-oriented novice, this is hard advice. It's being suggested that you spend countless hours in all kinds of weather so that you can bring in a few motley peas and a deformed squash. It is being suggested that you give up some of your TV time, your lying-on-the-couch time and other completely necessary endeavours so that you can bring in from the muck pile behind the badminton net a fraction of your annual food supply. If you wonder what this is all about, please take another look at chapter 1 "Why the Heck Should I Garden?" Then start looking at serious gardeners, wherever you may find them. Lots of them. The ones who are working on doing it right, who have unlined brows and happy countenances. They don't anger quickly and they have the patience of a rock. This seems to be what happens when you spend a lot of time adjusting to the vagaries of nature and watching the life cycles go by. You start feeling a bit more in tune with things, and more content with what life brings you. The mental health societies should take note and give out, perhaps, pea seeds, and a big warm smile, and a big welcome-back-to-the-planet as part of their opening protocol.

Naturally, all this seems simplistic from the opening gate of that meandering gardening path, and you still have that shrimpy little beginner's garden to nurse and protect and that can be a hard row to hoe, especially with Bill and Aunt Matty teasing you, but don't worry — you have a large support system and it spreads all around the world.

And you have my personal pride in you for starting the learning curve to garden, so much so that if you send me a letter describing your critical friend or relative I will send that person an explanatory request to give you a break. Because I think you're terrific, and so do many others.

You're just learning, for goodness' sake! Sheesh! Can't a person have some space to grow? You're helping to re-green the planet! You're starting on a new path! You're reducing greenhouse gas emissions! You're opening a new door in your brain! So here is a small gift to you — some tried and true wisdom to cheer you along!

# GLOSSARY OF TERMS

## Annual

A plant that carries out its whole life cycle in one year. These grow up from seeds, create flowers, put out seed pods and then die completely in winter. In spring, the seed begins the cycle again. Good examples of annuals are marigolds, peas, beans and petunias. As a complete, confusing aside, many plants we consider annual would actually live a lot longer if our winter climate didn't kill them off. Tomatoes will live through another summer if you bring them in and protect them all winter. Cabbage roots left in the ground may overwinter and produce new heads the next year. But telling you this might confuse you forever; forget I mentioned it.

## Bedding plants

The pretty but normally feeble and temporary plants that are put out in the spring for quick colour. They usually get eaten by slugs, need deadheading, and take up much of the world's peat bogs to produce in the first place. Since they don't have time to put down deep roots, they need a bit of feeding and watering to keep them alive. But apart from that, they are dandy things.

## Biennials

It's easy to memorize this term if you remember that "bi" means "two," which is why there are only two components to a bifold door. A biennial takes two years to complete its life cycle. In the first year, it grows up and establishes a nice strong root, then in winter it generally dies down. In the spring it puts on another push of growth from that good root and finally it grows a flower, gets pollinated, makes seeds and dies. The root usually dies then, too, and the cycle begins anew in the third year with the seeds germinating. Examples of biennials are parsley, carrots and caraway — generally many of the plants that put out a spoked, flat, umbrella-shaped flower head in the summer (the umbellifer).

## Blanch

To cover a plant part with soil or paper to keep the light out, so that the part will whiten and be more tender to eat. It's also called "blanching" when you quickly dip garden produce into boiling water before freezing it, so that the enzyme action stops quickly. Another form of blanching occurs to your face when you look out the window and see a raccoon eating corn on the cob — yours!

## Blight

The term "blight" is used freely and with conviction to describe any disease that makes your plants sick. You can stand beside any crinkled, blackened thing, nod your head knowingly and say "blight," and you will impress people and often be correct. Nothing to do about blight, really. Purchasing "blight-resistant" seeds from your catalogue, using mulch and praying frequently to the skies are the most scientific and proven methods for keeping this problem to a minimum.

## Bulb

Dry, papery-skinned bulbs look almost dead when they're still in the package. It's hard to believe that they are layers of leaves that enfold the flower bud you will be seeing in a few months. Our spring flowers such as tulips and daffodils come from bulbs. Bulbs are planted in late fall, like garlic, so that they will have a winter season to awake from and suddenly produce several leaves and a decorative flower. Then they begin to yellow and become floppy, but don't cut them down after the flower dies; the leaves need to gather the sun's energy to feed the bulb to start creating next year's flower and leaves. A cycle that's worth your cooperation!

## Compost

Any of the 31 methods of creating compost may be followed. The main ingredients should be garden waste, kitchen waste, comfrey leaves, animal waste, water and air. Sooner or later this will result in black gold, the best of garden food.

## Damping-off disease

Fungal spores drift through the air, and when they find the right setting (cool, damp) they "take," and your little plant seedlings will fall over and die. If you see this starting in your seed flats, try giving them more air movement, more heat and more light. I hear that a tea made from horsetail (the plant, silly!) will help with this. I use natural soil in my seedling beds and have very little damping-off, so you could try that.

## Deadheading

Some of these terms would frighten a normal person. Deadheading relates to a plant's never-ending need to produce seed (go forth and multiply, big time). The minute many plants have matured some seeds, they figure they've done their bit for plantdom, and promptly die. You can fool them by pinching off the flowers as they wither, usually down as far as the next bloom or tuft of greenery. The plant will then say "darn!" and crank out some more blooms. You certainly don't have to do this ('tain't natural), but it will give you more bloom time. It will also give you more peas and beans, since you are picking off the seed before it matures and it must now try to make more. Since the plant will have to put out more energy to produce these extra progeny (none of which will become a doctor), it's nice to give it a dose of manure tea to cheer it up.

## Deciduous

Plants either hold their leaves all year (evergreen) or lose them in the winter and grow them back in spring (deciduous). The way I remember this word is that the plant can't *decide* whether to have leaves or not, and that's all it takes to remember the full word. Usually. Well, often. Well …

## Dormant

Dormancy in plants is a lot like hibernation in bears. The plant is sleeping through winter and is avoiding the howling winds and the need to digest and utilize food. This is a good time to prune or move plants, because they won't get dehydrated, mostly because they don't have all that active growth to maintain but partly because their sap is running too slowly to bleed out. If you brought this plant into the warmth of your home, it would quickly "break dormancy" and begin to grow buds. If you brought a bear into the house, it would likely ruin the drapes. Don't ever do it.

## Drip line

This is the radio show you phone to complain about cranky people! Oh, sorry, I've been inhaling over the skullcap again. The term "drip line" is used to describe the outer ring that branches shade or cover around a tree or shrub. Imagine rain tumbling off the outermost leaves and creating an invisible circle around the tree trunk. The theory goes that a tree's most important roots are inside this drip line, so digging outside it is safe. It can be used for guessing where to begin digging up a tree, or feeding it.

## Evergreen

We know that evergreen trees don't lose their leaves (or, more likely, needles) in the winter, but there are a lot of garden plants that also retain theirs. If you make sure you have some evergreen plants around your door and yard, it won't look so dismal when everything else is dormant. Ivy, some honeysuckle, rhododendrons, a type of clematis vine, salal and periwinkle are a few examples of cheery winter types who do not ever give up.

## Fertilizer

My purist friends cringe when they hear that I use fertilizer on my plants — they think all fertilizers come out of those infamous boxes. But "to fertilize" to me means "to make fertile." I consider anything that makes my garden more fertile to be a fertilizer. So there!

## Hilling

The act of pushing soil up along a plant's stem so that it will be encouraged to put out more roots, and perhaps more root crops. But sometimes the purpose of hilling is to blanch. That's why I had to explain "blanch." You can hill soil along the stems of your leeks and it will blanch them (make them pale) by depriving them of light so that the chlorophyll heads for … greener pastures? Sorry!

## Intensive gardening

Several different schools of thought (French, double digging) suggest that deep digging and incorporation of great soil foods will give you a tremendous garden. And they're right! This is not suggested in this book because, well, it's … intensive. It takes energy and commitment, and if you weren't faint of heart you'd already be doing it.

## Manure tea

Actually, this could be "compost," "comfrey" or "seaweed" tea. Making tea is a way to turn a lump of manure, a bag of leaves or other awkward matter into a homogeneous, slow-release food that is easy to apply. Soaking plant matter breaks down the tissues, releasing the nutrients into the water. This can take several days. Manure that has hardened into a solid mass is easier to apply when it has been reduced to liquid form. My method is to keep a big plastic tub (mine is half of a giant apple juice barrel someone found floating in the ocean) and place it in a convenient spot in your garden. You won't want to move it later. When you receive a bag of rabbit manure or a handful

of comfrey leaves, throw them into this "soup" and let it fill with rainwater and sit in the sun. It will turn into a stinky mess and you can then stir it up, dip some into a bucket, fill the bucket with water (till the dilution looks like weak tea, but a bit stronger or weaker is fine) and throw this onto the garden. Any combination of manure, compost and plant matter will do, and you can simmer it like stock and then give everyone a good drink now and again. You can't really overfertilize this way, and it makes good use of foods that normally would take a long time to break down or be awkward to apply. There is a raging dispute about how long you should let it sit, but I have never heard a poor report about using old poo tea, so go ahead and make your own rules.

You will want to build a lid out of a hunk of wood for your barrel, because the mosquitoes will love that breeding brew if you give them access. A lid will also reduce the smell.

## Microclimates

If "climate" is something you have in your town, then a "microclimate" is something you have in your garden behind the garage — a tiny individual place with a definite sort of weather of its own. Behind the garage it is shady and cool, and in winter it freezes hard because the sun never hits it, and it takes a long time to warm up in the spring. But then it supports all sorts of lush weeds, unlike the dead, sunburned strip in front of the house — another microclimate altogether. Watch your garden for microclimates, and note them throughout the seasons so that you can match them with the best uses.

## Mulch

A layer of material to protect the soil from the sun's drying rays, and to weaken weed seeds as they sprout. Can be made of anything that will do the trick—old wool carpeting, cardboard, newspaper, hay, straw, leaves, etc. Make sure the soil is very moist before you apply a layer of mulch.

# Node

A place on a stem or branch that has the special capacity to put out new growth if need be. That is, if the top of a plant was suddenly snapped off by a passing Frisbee, the next remaining node would receive a chemical signal that it was now top dog and it would begin to put out a new branch or leaf. Many nodes just sit around waiting for this kind of thing to happen, which is about like the process for getting a promotion in my office, but more likely. Recognizing a node is good, because then you'll know what to cut back to when you're pruning, and what to look for when you're taking cuttings, or trying to encourage new growth.

# Permaculture
# (permanent agriculture)

Like forest gardening, the concept here is to plan layers of perennial plant life: a canopy of fruit trees, shrubs underneath, and shorter layers of herb and shade-loving plants at ground level. The result of arranging plants like this is to offer them a quite dynamic and companionable existence that extends all of their qualities. A very cool and ancient concept, well worth your future interest! Edible landscaping is its baby sister.

# Perennial

A plant that normally begins from a seed, but grows bigger each year. It may or may not die down to the soil each winter, but its root survives and grows, and when the root is sufficiently happy it begins popping out flowers each year. Rhubarb and artichokes are perennials, and so are lilies and hollyhocks.

# Pesticide

Anything with the suffix "-cide" is intended to kill the word in front of it. Therefore, herbicides kill plants, insecticides kill insects, etc. I always worry when I get my hair cut and I see the big jar of Barbercide on the desk, but obviously the rules of Latin do not apply at beauty salons. Pesticides can be made in a factory or created in your kitchen and all can be equally useful, except that the ones in your kitchen are almost always safer to handle, use, and inadvertently feed to the local waterways.

## Pollination

A seed, like the human ovum, doesn't get much chance to make a name for itself unless it gets pollinated. In the plant world, this can mean that the wind or an insect must bring pollen to the immature seed. For some plants this is very difficult, since only a single type of unusual moth is attracted to its particular scent (this is not where the term "wallflower" came from), but for other plants it's a ridiculously easy affair and bugs will carry pollen for miles around, pollinating everything in sight. Having lots of different flowers in your yard will ensure that the interested insects have plenty to keep them busy.

## Rhizome

A thickened piece of stem that turns sideways under the soil, runs horizontally and then grows roots. It can store food, adds stability to the plant, and can push out nodes from which new plants can grow straight up toward the light. Iris and bamboo have rhizomes.

## Root crops

If the main portion of your harvest is the part that grows underground, then it is a "root crop." These include potatoes, beets, parsnips and carrots, to name the most popular. Since it takes a long time to grow a big, healthy root (unless you are a radish, but let's not confuse things), most root crops are fall and winter foods. Because roots store water well and are technically still alive enough to start a new plant at a moment's notice, they keep well over winter or can be left in the garden for harvesting through to early spring.

## Rototilling

A rototiller is a machine with sharp little claws on the bottom that break up clumps of hardened soil. We've been conditioned to think that we need to use one of these each year to begin our spring garden but you can avoid battling with these heavy, stinky things (especially the part where you lift it gracefully out of the truck). If you have designated paths in your garden so that you aren't compacting your planting areas, and if you mulch carefully to keep the soil surface from crusting, you won't need to use a pollution-pumping machine any more. Besides, rototillers also break weed roots into many segments, all of which want to grow up big and strong. There is also a lot of controversy about whether "top" soil is meant for the top and bottom layers are meant to be on the bottom and the possibility that rototilling actually may be disturbing some ancient processes. At any rate, unless you're in a terrible hurry to get your garden going you can kiss that machine goodbye!

## Sterilized soil

The invention of "sterilized soil" is very new on the planet and nothing like it has ever supported a plant before. All plants have evolved in conjunction with a multitude of tiny organisms. When it was discovered that soil was carrying fungal spores that knocked down seedlings, someone chanced upon the cure of baking the soil to kill all organisms and weed seeds. You can sterilize your own soil if you like, or you can plant in plain old dirt like happened for the first 99 percent of our history. Try this experiment with two similar plants: put one in a pot of sterilized soil and the other in healthy garden soil or compost. Treat them the same. *Vive la différence!*

## Stewardship

My interpretation of this term is that instead of owning something like a tree, or our property, we instead act as "caregiver." We protect this piece of land from harm, we make room for its own rhythms and needs, and we recognize that it interacts with other yards and gardens and creatures and we make sure it can do this, while trying to gently glean what we need from it. This is being a good steward. The other kind of stewards hand out headphones on airplanes. They're good, too.

## Square foot gardening

Coined by Mel Bartholomew (author of the book, you guessed it, *Square Foot Gardening*), this term describes breaking your garden down into small chunks so you can tend them better. He literally gets us down to individual square feet so that we can arrange rotation of our plants effectively and give more attention to the bare spots. Read this book, but don't try to be perfect like him all at once.

## Sustainable

In relation to your garden, this means that the biomass within it can feed itself from its own dissolved parts (i.e., the same amount going in as coming out), with no outside sources of food being involved. Your garden then "sustains" itself. This takes a few years to get exactly right (see "The forest model" in chapter 3 for tips). You begin to live more "sustainably" when you find fewer ways to bring outside sources into your life, and instead find ways to reuse what is already present around you (reusing dishwater for the garden, using composting toilets, organic gardening).

## Thinning

When we scatter seeds, several may fall quite close together and begin to grow, resulting in a tiny clump of carrots or lettuce. The theory is that these will start competing for food and space, and that we should pluck out the smallest and weakest to let the mightier one live. The small, weak heart in me quails at the thought, so I do my thinning with a tiny, sharp stick and gently replant the smaller seedlings farther away in an empty space.

Once the seedlings get big enough to eat, thin them again, and this time the thinnings can go into the salad bowl.

## Top-dressing

Top-dressing, fortunately for me, has nothing to do with tying a scarf or I'd be sunk. Top-dressing entails laying a food material (such as compost, manure or seaweed) on the surface of the soil so that it can break down and wash in a natural, slow-release way. This is much easier than digging the fertilizing agent in, and will protect the soil surface from the elements.

## Transplanting

Moving a plant and its roots from point A to point B, be it out of one pot into a bigger one or out of a seed tray and into the garden.

## Viable

Alive, capable of growth. Sure, a plant can produce a lot of seed, but if it hasn't been pollinated or was badly stored it may not be viable.

## Weeding

The meditational action of removing unwanted plants from a garden area. You can do this in big, sweeps of your hand to keep them from seeding, or you can pluck out the tiny ones, making sure you have the roots in your hand. Weeds can be left on top of the mulch until the roots are dry and then shoved underneath to return their nutrients to the soil (of course, doing this when the plant has seeds on it is silly, unless you have a good mulch). Or you can leave the weeds in the ground and cover them with cardboard or hay to beat them down.

Conversely, you can find out what these weeds are and their other uses to humans. You can eat some of them (chickweed is good in salads and is very nutritious), you can make coffee extender out of others (dandelion roots), a quick

wound poultice out of burdock, etc. Blackberry leaves can be used for tea, and other plants provide edible roots and dyes. Get good mileage from your weeds by feeding them to your chickens or making "tea" for your garden. Borrow a book on native plants from your local library, and start looking at them with new eyes.

# FURTHER RESOURCES

## BOOKS

To create this list, I made a note of the books that I lend out most or open up to show a page to an interested beginner. These books make for a nice gardening library.

Bartholomew, Mel
*Square Foot Gardening*, Emmaus, PA, Rodale Press, 1981.
Full of so many useful tips.

Bremness, Lesley
*The Complete Book of Herbs*, New York, Viking Studio Books, 1988.
Everything you wanted to know about herbs but were afraid to ask.

Fukuoka, Masanobu
*The Natural Way of Farming*, Tokyo, Japan Publications, 1985.
I suggest the *Natural Way of Farming* only to those who are no longer faint of heart, as its combination of political and philosophical ingredients may be heavy going for the new grower. Definitely rich with concepts, though, and the guiding light for a lot of us.

Emery, Carla
*The Encyclopedia of Country Living*, Seattle, Sasquatch Books, 1994.
Soap making, chicken farming, rice growing, olive producing, wood chopping … a favorite standby. A real "everything you wanted to know" book, and worth every penny.

Flowerdew, Bob
*Bob Flowerdew's Complete Fruit Book*, Vancouver, Raincoast Books, 1997.
Basic cultivation and pruning tips for an amazing assortment of edible shrubs and trees.

Hupping, Carol, ed.
*Stocking Up*, Emmaus, PA, Rodale Press, 1986.
How to extend the shelf life of your nuts, fruit, grain and other perishable harvest, using every conceivable method.

Jason, Dan
*Greening the Garden: A Guide to Sustainable Growing*, Gabriola Island, B.C., New Society Publishers, 1991.
An introduction to the political importance of what we eat and where we get it, with descriptions of lots of foods we can grow ourselves and how to cook them. Dan writes good books that teach people to live sustainably.

Meuninck, Jim
*The Basic Essentials of Edible Wild Plants and Useful Herbs*, Merrillville, IN, ICS Books Inc., 1988.
Understand and make use of the native plants growing around your area.

Ody, Penelope
*The Complete Medicinal Herbal*, Toronto, Key Porter Books, 1993.
The best all round book I've seen on creating herbal medications. Clear descriptions and good identifying photographs.

Parnes, Robert, *The Fertile Soil*, Davis, CA, AgAccess, 1990.
Finally, someone has produced scientific evidence so that we can compare the nutrients of many available materials. Hard slogging for beginners, but full of interesting facts.

Pavord, Anna
*The New Kitchen Garden*, North Vancouver, B.C., Cavendish Books, 1996.
Plant descriptions and uses, companion gardening and recipes. Pretty pictures.

*Sunset Western Garden Book*
(various authors), Mehlo Park, CA, Sunset Publishing Corporation, 1998.
Good descriptions of how to look after a huge range plants, including most of our common garden plants. No photos, only illustrations, but you may be able to identify your plants from the descriptions.

Turner, Nancy J.
*Food Plants of Coastal First Peoples,* Vancouver, UBC Press, 1995.
An excellent book for identifying edible plants, investigating shade plants for your yard and learning about the huge range of foods growing right in front of you.


# RECOMMENDED CATALOGUES

**Salt Spring Seeds**
Box 444, Ganges Post Office
Salt Spring Island, BC
V8K 2W1
Phone: (250) 537-5269
All the seeds mentioned in *Greening the Garden* are found here, guaranteed non-biologically engineered and pure of heart. If you eat from this catalogue you will be healthy, and so will the planet. Send owner Dan Jason thanks for saving all these seeds!

**West Coast Seeds**
8475 Ontario Street
Vancouver, BC
V5X 3E8
Phone: (604) 482-8800
Fax: (877) 482-8822
email: info@westcoastseeds.com
A great example of a seed catalogue that acts as a planting guide. Keep this in your bookcase as a year-round resource. (If you wish to learn seed saving, remember to buy only open-pollinated seeds.)

# INTERNET

I'm not much of an Internet user, but I do love being able to pull catalogues and general information into my living room whenever I want. There's just so much of it out there! So here is a very small list of sites for you to check out — either to find seeds or to learn more about backyard gardening. Just follow the links when you decide that you want more!

- www.grimonut.com — Grimo Nut Nursery, based in Niagara-on-the-Lake, Ontario, provides some of the best, most hardy nut trees, tree products and nut products

- www.oldgrowth.org/compost/ — Compost Resource Page is intended to serve as a hub of information for anyone interested in the various aspects of composting

- www.rain.org/~philfear/garden.html — Gardening as an Anarchist Plot offers information on how to grow your own food and medicine in a small organic garden the size of a bedroom. Companion planting, intensive beds, potato barrels and more

- www.saltspring.com/ssseeds/ — Salt Spring Seeds promotes self-empowerment by providing untreated seeds to grow high-protein, good yielding and great tasting crops

- www.seeds.ca — Seeds of Diversity Canada is a non-profit group of gardeners from coast to coast who save seeds from rare and unusual garden plants for the purpose of preserving the varieties

- www.thesavagegarden.com — The Savage Garden is an organic gardening resource site for gardeners by gardeners

- www.westcoastseeds.com — West Coast Seeds is a user-friendly site with real humans who can answer your questions. A good selection of most of the usual garden veggie seeds as well as other products

# ACKNOWLEDGEMENTS

Even light-hearted gardening books aren't written without emotional support, role models, garden gurus and someone to make the soup.

My thanks to Lawrence Henrey, the mystery scientist, and to Naturescape British Columbia for the butterfly and hummingbird list. I bow to Peter Light and Bill Mollinson for knowing how to live in their gardens and to Masanobu Fukuoka for shifting the revolution back to where it should be. Many thanks to Diane Nicholson, the Salad Queen and another great role model, for always offering her knowledge to everyone for free.

Every budding author needs a friend who runs down the driveway to throw on a pot of soup and grab the laundry so that we can pound the keyboard uninterrupted and meet the next deadline — thanks, Janet Whitfield, for your unending belief in this project.

And huge bouquets of gratitude to Kathryn Graydon and family, and Cindy Sutherland for timely and unrelenting support.

My thanks to Elaine Jones for teaching me I could "fight back" with an editor, and to Derek Fairbridge for letting me practise on him, and for his very deft hand on the editorial pruning shears.

Big thanks to Suzy Naylor for putting this project back on the trail when I was ready to let it go, and of course to Frank Henning for getting the seed planted by saying, "Hey — why don't you write a book?"

And to my crazy but loving family who always make room for my perhaps mystifying career choices. I am sorry to tell you, I am not done yet! But thanks for the great computer stuff, Mom and Dad — it really came in handy! And thanks, sisters, for your faith.

And thanks to all the rest of you who said this book was going to make it – you have been the "poo tea" for my soul — may your gardens abound!

# INDEX